THE
HONOREE

WOLE ADEYEMI

ISBN: 978-1-964289-50-2

DEDICATION AND ACKNOWLEDGMENTS

I'd like to thank countless people for their help in my life. Without them, I won't be who I am neither would I have done what I did.

To all the wonderful people I wrote about, thank you for your permission. I hope you would find satisfaction in this acknowledgement.

Finally, my fantastic readers, I am indebted to you, too.

Table of Contents

PROLOGUE

After discussing with the school management, our parents gave their consent for Ebun to visit China. Although we were both envious of her that she alone was going to China, we knew that she had earned it, so we were happy for her. The school made all the preparations. When she was leaving, the school had a small ceremony for her where she was praised by her teachers and principal; She was given a shield, too.

Ebun was not the only gem in her school; her classmate Stacy was the runner-up in this competition. She chose to write on inequality, and her topic was "Sharing of Wealth through a Wealth Tax." In her paper, she wrote that 0.003 percent of Nigerians have 1.4 times more wealth than 107 million other Nigerians. According to her, this was far from fair, and she had a solution for that.

She proposed that if the government imposes different taxes on rich people, billions of dollars could be raised. She suggested that a wealth tax of 2% on millionaires, 3% on people who had more than $20 million, and 5% on Nigerians with wealth above $50 million should be imposed. This way, $3.2 billion could be saved every year, and this amount could be spent on healthcare, which could double what the government spends normally

"I am calling on more tax on billionaires than on workers. I'd like to send this message not only to the Nigerian government but to all world leaders. Thank you so much," Stacy ended her speech. She received a grand applause for it and was then given a big bouquet, a gift hamper, and a shield.

Ebun was among those applauding Stacy. She was on cloud nine, and her friends were equally happy for her. Ife clapped the loudest when Ebun was on stage. Our parents stood with the other parents, and they were teary- eyed.

The day when Ebun was to leave for China finally came. It was the first time she would travel alone and her first time to travel abroad. She had fun and made friends on her flight. When the flight crew knew that she was the winner of the competition, they offered her a tour of the cockpit.

Her plane touched down at Beijing airport at dawn. Meanwhile, two teachers from her school accompanied her on her trip. It was a cold day and Ebun loved it. She stayed in a 5-star hotel in Beijing and enjoyed a lavish menu. When she got to her suite, she called us through her laptop and showed us what it looked like.

She sat before her laptop and had a big grin when we appeared on the screen. She waved excitedly at us and felt a pang of homesickness as she saw our faces.

"Hi, Ebun! How's China?" Ife asked, her eyes wide with curiosity.

"It's amazing!" Ebun replied, beaming. "I will see so many cool places like the Great Wall and the Forbidden City."

"Wow!" Ife exclaimed. "I wish I could come with you."

"Yeah, it's not fair that you get to have all the fun," I added, pouting playfully.

Ebun laughed. "Sorry guys, I'll bring back lots of souvenirs for you."

"Speaking of souvenirs, have you bought anything for us yet?" Mum chimed in humorously.

Ebun rolled her eyes. "Mum, I just got here. I haven't had time to go shopping yet."

"Well, you are not allowed inside this house unless you get us souvenirs," Ife said threateningly as she nibbled on her bar of chocolate.

"Sure, sure. Have faith, OK?" Ebun said, rolling her eyes.

"We are just teasing you, baby. We miss you loads. When are you coming back home?" Mum asked, emotions written over her face. "I'll be back in a few days," Ebun replied, trying to sound reassuring. "I promise I'll return with lots of stories to tell."

"We can't wait to hear them," General Akin Olokun-Esin said with a smile on his face.

"Me too," Ife added.

Ebun felt a warm glow of happiness fill her chest. Although she was far from home, she knew that her family was always there for her.

She told us she couldn't wait to see us again and recount her amazing trip.

Ebun had lunch later and video-called Ann and Lisa. Since she had a tiring flight, she had an early night's rest. Her teachers woke her up early the next morning and told her that she would be visiting one of the best schools in Beijing. There, she would meet students who wrote on the same topic she wrote about. These students will also visit Nigeria soon.

Ebun told me about her experience on the school tour. She was astonished by how technologically advanced the schooling system was in China. The students had electronic books, and every class had a projector for the teacher to teach the students optimally. Ebun conversed with students there and got to know about their culture. Everyone loved her, and they were impressed by her knowledge. She was amazed by how far she had come.

She vowed to work harder so she could travel and learn more about different cultures and countries.

Ebun was given a tour of important places in Beijing and went to see the Great Wall of China. She took pictures there and marvelled at one of the Seven Wonders of the World. She was also taken to the Forbidden City, after which she visited the famous 798 Art Zone - which I had told her about - followed by a hearty meal at the Tribe Solana Restaurant.

Tribe Solana is a great restaurant for health-conscious families looking to keep their kids entertained, as there is a fun play area for little ones like

Ebun. The restaurant boasts a Western-styled children's menu, too. It focuses on healthy food and caters to all diet restrictions.

After spending a week in Beijing, Ebun was told that she would be travelling to Shanghai. She was excited about the news because she would be taken to DisneyLand as a reward for writing one of the best papers in the competition. She was having the time of her life.

When she got to Shanghai Disney Resort, she was awestruck. She had never been to an amusement park that big. She spent the day with her favourite Disney characters and watched the parade while dancing to all her favourite classic Disney numbers. She even got

to enjoy all of the Pixar and Marvel joy rides. No doubt that she had a swell time.

By the time she had enjoyed all the attractions, she was tired and slept off in the car on her ride back to her hotel room while clutching an Iron Man plush toy she won in a ring toss game.

Ebun woke up the next day later than usual. To her surprise, her teachers told her that they were taking her to Shanghai's amazing Ocean Aquarium. Although she was afraid of the sea and big fish, she still went on the tour. She was curious to see those sea creatures up close.

She was scared to enter the glass tunnel with fish swimming around her. Watching sharks so close gave her the creeps, but her teachers assured her that she was safe. She felt relieved by their assurance and enjoyed her time there. Afterwards, they went to the Magic Funhouse, which was mind-boggling and entertaining. She saw all kinds of 3D art, murals, and sculptures and was impressed by all the creativity that surrounded her.

"OK, Sweetie, time to go now; the staff are closing up the space," Ebun's teachers told her as the staff ushered out all the visitors.

"We still have so much to see. Why is everyone leaving?" Ebun asked innocently.

"Sweetie, there is an outbreak of a disease, so they are closing up all public spaces so many people don't get infected. That is why we have to leave," one of her teachers told Ebun in a worried tone.

Ebun's excitement was cut short by this sad news and it was replaced with worry. When she got out of the Fun House, she saw people running around and wearing masks. The whole place was filled with panic. She recalled the memory of the dream she had back home and became scared.

"I want to go home!" she flatly told her teachers, who were busy collecting masks from a health worker stationed outside.

"In time, Sweetie. Wear this and do not take it off under any condition, OK?" she told Ebun. Ebun nodded reluctantly, her heart pounding.

They returned to their hotel and remained inside for the next four days. Ebun discovered, through the news, that a pandemic (COVID-19 virus) had hit the country and people all over were dying as a result.

CHAPTER 1

AANU

G rowing up in Nigeria, I was always amazed by the remarkable ability of Nigerians to embrace people from diverse ethnic backgrounds. As the most populous country in Africa and the largest democracy on the continent, Nigeria boasts a staggering number of ethnic groups, surpassing 300, each with its unique cultural identities and over 500 languages spoken among these diverse ethnic nationalities. This diversity is truly awe-inspiring and serves as a constant reminder of the rich tapestry of cultures that make up our great nation.

One of the things that fill me with immense pride is how Nigeria has embraced individuals from various cultures and made them feel at home. This attests to the spirit of inclusivity and acceptance that runs deep within our national identity. Whether someone comes from a neighbouring African country or a faraway land, Nigeria always accommodates and integrates them into society.

The three major ethnic groups in Nigeria, often called the tripod of the nation, are the Hausa-Fulani, Yoruba, and Igbo ethnic groups. Each of these groups bring their unique traditions, customs, and languages that further enrich the cultural fabric of our country. The Hausa-Fulani ethnicity, with a strong Islamic heritage, is predominantly found in the Northern region. The Yoruba people, known for their vibrant art, literature, and music, are primarily located in the Southwestern part of the country, while the Igbo, renowned for their entrepreneurial spirit and rich cultural practices, are mainly concentrated in the Southeastern regions.

These three major ethnic groups, along with numerous other smaller ethnic nationalities, coexist harmoniously and respect one another's differences while celebrating their shared values. Despite the occasional challenges that arise from our diverse backgrounds, Nigeria has continually demonstrated a commitment to unity, striving to foster a sense of national identity that transcends ethnic boundaries.

Our cultural diversity not only shapes our traditions and ways of life but also serves as a source of inspiration and pride. From the colourful festivals and ceremonies that showcase our various ethnic heritages to the mouth- watering array of cuisines representing different regions, Nigeria is a treasure trove of cultural experiences.

As I reflect on the remarkable tapestry of cultures that comprise Nigeria, I am grateful for the opportunities to learn, grow, and appreciate the beauty of our diversity. This very diversity binds us together as a nation, enabling us to face challenges with resilience, creativity, and a deep understanding of one another.

Our ability to embrace and celebrate our cultural diversity is not just a point of pride; it is a testament to our nation's strength and resilience. Our collective heritage is a foundation upon which we can build a better future, one that upholds the values of inclusivity, acceptance, and unity. I am grateful to belong to a country that cherishes its multicultural heritage and remains committed to forging a path forward as a nation that stands tall in its diversity.

In our fourth-grade class, I had classmates from different ethnic nationalities around the world. It was an enriching experience that broadened their horizons and fostered cultural understanding. Our classroom was like a mini United Nations, filled with a vibrant diversity of traditions, languages, and customs.

Ife and I used to sit together in the second row while Ebun sat on the first desk in the front row. Next to Ebun was Antonella, whose Latin American heritage shone through her proud demeanour. She shared stories of her family's traditions and customs and told us about culturally rich aspects of her homeland. It was fascinating to learn about the naming conventions in her country, where children bore the surnames of both parents. This practice highlighted the importance of honouring both lineages and celebrating family ties.

Across the room, there was Jessica, who was British. She shared her uncle's remarkable journey. Her uncle, Pierre Fatumbi Verger, was a French photographer and researcher who found a second home in Nigeria. Through his lens, he captured the lives and stories of the Oyo people, showcasing their beauty, tenacity, and dynamic culture. Her tales of her uncle's experiences emphasised the welcoming nature of our country and how we embrace individuals who seek to explore and appreciate our prolific heritage.

In other classes, I also had mates from different ethnic groups within Nigeria. They celebrated the diversity of their country, with students representing Yoruba, Igbo, Hausa, and many other ethnic nationalities. Each person brought their unique perspectives, languages, and traditions that fostered a sense of unity and understanding among them.

Ebun's classroom was a microcosm of Nigeria's larger society. The streets of our cities are alive with the sounds of different languages, the aromas of diverse cuisines, and the colours of various traditional attires. Nigeria has always been a melting pot of cultures where people from different backgrounds can thrive and contribute to our collective growth.

Being surrounded by classmates from different ethnic backgrounds broadened our worldview and instilled in us a deep appreciation for cultural diversity. We exchanged stories, and shared our favourite traditional dishes, and celebrated each other's festivals. It was a beautiful mosaic of cultures that enhanced our educational journey and taught us the value of embracing our differences.

The hot mornings in May that heralded the beginning of the rainy season filled the air with a sense of anticipation as Ebun walked into her fourth-grade classroom. Her teacher, Mrs Shirley Paine, had given the students an intriguing assignment. They were to write an essay on the importance of their family names. Ebun was excited about the opportunity to delve into her own family's history and explore the significance behind her name.

After two weeks of researching, writing, and pouring her heart into her essay, the moment of truth arrived. She and her classmates were supposed to present their essays according to the alphabetical listing of their names. Soon, it was the turn of one of her good friends Antonella to present her essay. She belonged to a Hispanic household, and her family values were deeply rooted in her behaviour. Ebun sat up straight, intrigued by the the topic she had chosen. Antonella confidently walked to the front of the class and greeted everyone with a warm smile.

"Hi, friends," she began with enthusiasm. "My name is Antonella Jose Diego, and I have two surnames; one belongs to my mother, and the other to my father, and that is the main topic of my essay."

As she introduced herself, Ebun couldn't help but admire the way both her surnames rolled off her tongue, each one representing a distinct lineage. She was fascinated by the significance behind her name, and she anticipated what she had to share.

Antonella proceeded to enlighten her classmates about the tradition of giving babies two last names in Latin America. She highlighted countries, such as Chile, Spain, and Mexico, which adopted this naming convention. She mentioned that Italy recently embraced it, too.

"In these countries," she explained, "everyone has two surnames. It is a long-standing tradition that holds great cultural significance. When a child is born, they are given their father's surname, followed by their mother's paternal surnames."

Her words transported her classmates to a world where names were carefully crafted to honour both the maternal and paternal lineages. It is a beautiful way to acknowledge the importance of both parents and their families in a person's identity.

Antonella then turned our attention to the variations in naming conventions across different countries. She mentioned that hyphenated last names were more widely accepted in the United States as they provided a solution for couples with hyphenated last names themselves. However, she pointed out that figuring out which names to pass down could become quite messy in such cases.

"Contrastingly," she continued, "double-barrelled surnames can also retain the patrilineal lineage of their own. In Spain, for example, it is required that the father's last name be listed first. This ensures that it becomes the next name passed down when genealogists and historians research Spanish- surnamed ancestors and families.

"Here is a fun fact: In Spanish-speaking countries, the naming convention of the Nile River remains the same as in other languages. The Nile is known as "el Nilo" in Spanish. The name "Nilo" originates from the Latin word "Nilus," which was derived from the Greek word "Neilos."

"The Nile River is a significant geographical feature, flowing through several countries in Africa, including Sudan, South Sudan, Ethiopia, Uganda, and Egypt. It is the longest river in Africa and one of the longest rivers in the world.

"In Spanish, when referring to the Nile, it is common to use the definite article "el" before the name, as in "el Nilo.

The naming convention of the Nile River in Spanish-speaking countries aligns with the general usage of the term "el Nilo" to refer to this iconic African river," Antonella added with a smile and thanked the class before returning to her seat.

The entire class was impressed by Antonella's knowledge of languages, naming traditions and her ability to articulate their nuances. It was as if she had taken us (her classmates) on a journey through different cultures, opening our eyes to the intricacies of identity and heritage.

As she concluded her essay, Antonella left her classmates with a greater appreciation for the diversity of naming practices worldwide. It reminded us that names hold stories, histories, and connections to our families and ancestors. The whole class applauded her passionately and acknowledged the depth of her research and the insight she had shared.

In that moment, Ebun realised how fortunate she was to be a part of a class where each person brought their own unique experiences and cultural backgrounds. They were not just learning about essays and academic subjects but also gaining a deeper understanding of the world and the people within it. Antonella's essay not only educated them but also fostered a sense of unity and respect for the rich tapestry of names that surrounded them.

After Antonella finished presenting her essay, Mrs Paine stood before the class and said, "I am happy to announce that Ebun's paper was the most outstanding. Let's have a round of applause for Ebun!"

Ebun's heart swelled with pride as her teacher called her up to the front of the class. As she stood there, clutching her paper titled "The meaning, importance, and praise poetry of my family name - Olokun-Esin," she felt both nervous and excited. She began to read her paper, her voice echoing throughout the room as the words she had meticulously crafted rang in the ears of her classmates.

Little did she know that among her classmates was Jessica Verger, whose uncle, Pierre Fatumbi Verger, had once lived in Nigeria and documented the lives of the Oyo people, particularly during the reign of Alaafin Siyanbola Ladigbolu. His dedication to capturing the beauty and dignity of the African culture through his photography left a lasting impact.

Jessica approached Ebun after the class, her eyes shining with excitement.

"Hey, Ebun! I have something really special to share with you about Pierre Fatumbi Verger. You may already know this, but I wanted to take a moment to tell you about his remarkable work. He was my uncle," Jessica said.

"He was your uncle?!" Ebun asked her, genuinely surprised.

"Yes! My uncle devoted his entire life to studying Africa and the African diaspora across the world. He had a deep passion for understanding the enduring connections between the people and cultures of West Africa and the African diaspora. It's amazing how he went beyond just studying Africa but also extended his research to explore the links that unite these communities," Jessica said in a flurry of words. She was clearly beyond excited to share with Ebun.

"Wow. You must be incredibly proud of him!" Ebun said.

"He is my inspiration! What's truly remarkable is that for over five decades, he took approximately 65,000 photographs using his beloved Rolleiflex camera. Can you imagine the dedication and effort it took to create such a vast collection? Each photograph attested to his passion and commitment.

"His approach to photography was truly unique. He focused on humanistic light-filled portraits that portrayed individuals and groups in the most beautiful and dignified ways possible. He aimed to emphasise the beauty of the human form in everyday life. This was how he countered the prevalent derogatory and racially biased representations of Africans and people of African descent during the 20th century," Jessica said proudly.

"Such a great guy! I am sure he must have been a great human being, too, with the level of empathy and understanding he showed," Ebun said admiringly.

"Exactly! My family said that he was the nicest guy you'd meet. He took those photographs to challenge those harmful stereotypes and showcase the true richness and dignity of the communities he captured. He wanted to change the narrative and highlight the enduring connections between people and cultures," Jessica said.

Ebun could see the shine in Jessica's eyes as she talked about her uncle.

"Jess, you have every reason to be incredibly proud of your uncle's work," Ebun said with the brightest smile. "He was an inspiring figure who used his art to make a positive impact on how Africans and people of African descent were represented. His dedication to studying and celebrating the African diaspora is truly remarkable, and trust me; I am so grateful for his contribution and truly honoured to be your friend."

Jessica shared stories of her uncle's work and promised to provide Ebun with materials, including photographs of the Oyo people. True to her word, seven days later, a package arrived from the Pierre Verger Foundation in Brazil. It contained dozens of sound recordings, video films, and photographs of Oyo people.

Ebun was wowed when she saw that Pierre Fatumbi Verger managed to capture one of the rarest sights: the picture of Alaafin Siyanbola Ladigbolu and the last Olokun-Esin or Abobaku. It was truly extraordinary to have a visual record of such significant figures.

It seemed that Alaafin Siyanbola Ladigbolu witnessed the end of the ritual suicide of the Olokun-Esin. During the celebration of the Alaafin's ritual in 1946, a unique circumstance surrounded the role of the Abobaku. Although the previous Alaafin had passed away in 1944, it required the intervention of a British officer to save the life of the designated Abobaku, as recorded in Professor *Wole Soyinka's play Death and the King's Horseman.*

It was fascinating how the British officer played a crucial role in this situation. By putting one Abobaku, who was meant to commit suicide and be buried alongside the departed Alaafin, in jail, he effectively prevented the tragic fate of the chosen individual.

Ebun was full of gratitude to Jessica. Having such a photograph in Pierre Fatumbi Verger's collection was truly exceptional. It served as a historical record, capturing a significant moment and shedding light on the cultural practices of that time. Ebun could gain a deeper understanding of the rituals and traditions that shaped the history of her people only through such photographs.

The class gathered around as Ebun played the sound recordings, which featured people speaking Yoruba. My sisters, Ebun and Ife, and I took turns translating the words to the delight of our classmates. We were privileged to be taught Yoruba by our parents and it opened up a world of understanding and connection.

At that moment, the importance of the mother tongue became clear. The language formed the foundation of our thinking and emotions. It connected us to our culture and ensured enhanced cognitive development. Our ability to translate the recordings not only delighted our classmates but also emphasised the significance of preserving and embracing our native language.

As the days went by, Ebun continued to explore her passion for writing through online creative writing programs, thanks to her friend Stacy. Her summer classes adequately prepared Ebun for future essays and nurtured her love for storytelling.

As the hot summer days continued, Ebun eagerly looked forward to the adventures that awaited her. She was armed with the power of words to connect, inspire, and heal.

Curious children will own and build the future. These children aren't scared to experiment, investigate, prod, inquire, and turn things inside out. My little sister Ebun was a curious kid. She had begun to explore her surroundings since she started walking on her two little feet. Sometimes, she would get in trouble for being too curious. Meanwhile, if a mother could ask for a priceless gift for her child, she would ask God to endow her child with curiosity.

Today, we have access to a wealth of information and resources through the internet and search engines that were not available to previous generations. With online learning, we can access educational materials from around the world, learn at our own pace, and interact with experts and other learners from different cultures and backgrounds. This has enabled us to develop a broader and more diverse knowledge base and skillset our parents didn't have at our age.

Also, advances in science and technology have made it possible for us children to learn about complex topics and concepts earlier in our lives than in the past. For example, nowadays children are introduced to programming and robotics quite early, which can help them develop critical thinking and problem-solving skills.

I am fascinated by how today's children seem to possess a level of wisdom, intelligence, and knowledge that surpasses what their parents had at their age. It's truly remarkable to witness how they navigate the world and act in surprising ways. Reflecting on this, I believe several key factors contribute to their remarkable capabilities.

Firstly, today's children have the power of search engines at their fingertips. They are more independent about learning new things. Rather than constantly pester their parents for answers to their questions, which their parents may not even know, they can simply log on to a search engine and find information on their own. This access to an array of knowledge empowers them to explore and learn in ways that were not possible for previous generations.

Another significant aspect of their reality is the augmentation of their learning experiences. Children today are exposed to audio-visual aids that enhance their understanding and how they retain information. From interactive educational videos to virtual reality simulations, they have access to lots of multimedia resources that make learning more engaging and immersive.

Additionally, children are effectively gamifying their learning experiences. Imagine solving math riddles while competing in real-time with children from another country, with the possibility of winning a prize. This interactive and competitive approach to learning makes it more enjoyable and encourages them to actively participate and excel in their studies.

When I was their age, I relied on the books my parents bought me or the limited selection available at the school or public library. Today, children have the incredible advantage of the internet and e-books. They can access thousands of books and resources at the same cost as a library membership, opening up a world of knowledge and endless learning possibilities.

Furthermore, children today often have access to personal tutors. These tutors are not only human but also bots online! They cater to their individual needs and learning styles. This personalised guidance and support significantly enhances their educational journey and helps them reach their full potential.

Thanks to technological advancements, children can now connect with important people in their lives regardless of distance. Platforms like *Skype* and *Facebook* allow them to maintain close relationships with their role models, even if they live on different continents. This level of connectivity was unimaginable for us when we were growing up and has undoubtedly had a profound impact on their development.

There are no limitations on the time available for learning. While schools and libraries used to have strict opening and closing hours, children today can continue their learning journey whenever they have access to a personal computer, an internet connection, and electricity. Whether it's day or night, a weekend or a weekday, they can learn and explore their interests without constraints.

Today's children possess a unique advantage in terms of knowledge and learning capabilities. The availability of search engines, augmented reality, gamified learning, access to vast digital resources, personalised tutoring, easy connection to role models, and the flexibility of learning anytime have all contributed to their exceptional abilities. As they continue to grow and develop, I can only imagine the incredible achievements they will accomplish and the positive impacts they will have on our ever-evolving world.

My name is Aanu, and I have two younger sisters. We were triplets, a truly remarkable bond. It began when I was snugly tucked away in my mother's womb, enjoying the cosy darkness and blissfully unaware of the world outside. Little did I know that a hilarious mix-up was about to unfold.

You see, the doctors relied on X-rays to peek inside my mother's womb and get a glimpse of our developing bodies. Now, X-rays are usually pretty handy tools that allow doctors to spot all sorts of things without resorting to surgery. But then, even the most seasoned doctors can sometimes misinterpret those tricky images.

In our case, those sneaky X-rays played a little prank on the radiologists. They told our parents that there were just two of us happily coexisting in our mom's womb. Twins! Imagine how surprised our parents were when, after eight months, they discovered that we were three bundles of joy, not two. Triplets!

You can only imagine the laughter and confusion that followed! Despite the amazing advancements in radiological science, those X-rays can sometimes play tricks on the best of radiologists. You'll be right to say the late discovery caught everyone off guard and added an unexpected twist to our family tale.

Now, while this misdiagnosis might have caused a bit of chaos at first, it certainly didn't dampen our parents' joy and excitement. If anything, it tripled it! We were welcomed into the world as an extraordinary surprise, and our family's love grew threefold.

So, you see, even in the world of medicine, where science and technology reign, there's always room for a good of mix-up. Life has a funny way of surprising us. In our case, it came with an extra dose of togetherness. We may have started as a misread X-ray, but we are living proof that even the greatest surprises can bring immeasurable happiness.

What fascinates me the most is the unique genetic makeup of my sisters and me. There are two types of triplets: trizygotic or fraternal triplets and identical or monozygotic triplets. Interestingly, around 80% or more of triplets belong to the fraternal variety.

In our case, Ife and I are identical twins; we share an extraordinary resemblance. At times, our physical features, mannerisms, and even our laughter are almost indistinguishable. This bond is a special connection that we cherish.

On the other hand, Ebun, our beloved sister, was the fraternal triplet. She had her distinct features, a uniqueness that set her apart. While being a trio already makes us unique, Ebun always stands out as the most precocious and creative of us all.

From an early age, it was clear that Ebun possessed a remarkable intellect and curiosity. She seemed to have an innate thirst for knowledge and a natural inclination to explore the world around her. While my other sister and I were content with playing with toys, Ebun was always questioning everything, seeking answers, and coming up with innovative ideas.

Her creativity knows no bounds. She has this amazing ability to take ordinary objects and turn them into extraordinary works of art. Give her a box of crayons and she would transform it into a magical world on paper. Hand her a pile of Legos and she would build the most intricate and imaginative structures you could imagine. Her mind has always been a playground of ideas, and she delights in sharing her creations with anyone who would lend an ear.

However, not only Ebun's artistic talents set her apart. She had an insatiable appetite for learning and a knack for understanding complex concepts right from childhood. While my other sister and I struggled with math problems, Ebun would effortlessly solve them. She would solve advanced equations before we could wrap our heads around the basics.

She was a voracious reader, so she devoured books faster than our parents could supply them. It seemed like she had a huge library stored in her mind, and she would often regale us with fascinating tales and interesting facts that she had picked up along the way. Her imagination fuelled her love for storytelling. She would captivate us with her original narratives and transport us to faraway lands and magical realms.

However, what truly made Ebun special was her kind heart and infectious enthusiasm. Wherever she goes, she uplifts those around her and spreads joy and laughter. Her genuine care for others, combined with her creative spirit, makes her a beloved friend to many. She is always there with a comforting word, a helping hand, or a brilliant idea to solve any problem.

As we grew older, Ebun's uniqueness became more pronounced. Her talents blossomed and she pursued her passions with unwavering determination. Whether it was painting, writing, or delving into scientific experiments, she threw herself into every endeavour with a fervour that inspired us all.

As triplets, we shared an incredible bond, but we also celebrated our individuality.

We each bring our perspectives and strengths to the table through this beautiful diversity. We have always complemented and supported one another, and that makes our bond as triplets even stronger.

We lived with our father, General Akin Olokun-Esin, who was an army man and our mum, Mrs Olokun-Esin, who loved us dearly. She loved to cook and recite *oriki* in her sweet voice every morning. Every morning, as the sun gently caressed our room, my sisters and I would wake up to the soothing voice of our mum reciting our *oriki Olokun-Esin*. It was a beautiful ritual that connected us to our ancestors and filled us with a sense of pride and strength.

One day, inspired by the power of words in an audio music disc our father had, we decided to share a line from A Strong Man's *oriki* with our classmates. It went like this: "You stroll through the city and return with an abundance of fowls like a prophet. You do not buy; you do not snatch; you do not steal. Not one of the fowls are given to you; the fowls are only ill-fated!" My classmates burst into laughter because they found the line both amusing and intriguing. What a portrayal of the political juggernaut, called an elephant who disturbingly trembles the equilibrium of western Nigerian politics! They each offered their interpretations of its meaning, adding to the joyous atmosphere.

Ebun seized the moment to explain to our classmates that besides our first names, we also had two other names called *oriki*. They were special names and held deep meanings. She shared examples of female oriki names such as Asake, Abeke, Arike, Aduke, Anike, Ajoke, Asunle, and Ajike. Males have names like Akanbi, Alabi, Ajagbe, Adio, Alagbe, Ayinde, Ayinla, and more. These names carried significant symbolism and represented the values and aspirations of our families.

There were Muslim students from around the world in our class as well: Quadria was an Egyptian; Hoda was a classmate from Saudi Arabia; Daria was Iranian, and Alara was a cute Turkish girl with cat-like features. They were all surprised at the idea of having multiple names.

"Aanu, would it be considered offensive or confusing for one person to have so many different names?" Hoda asked me as Quadria, Daria, and Alara listened curiously.

"In the Yoruba culture, it's not offensive to have multiple names; instead, it is a celebration of our identity. Names hold great importance for us; they reflect our heritage, beliefs, and the hopes our parents have for us."

Hoda then shared her cultural perspective.

"In our religion, parents are not allowed to give their babies compound or improper names. Islam strictly states that the names given to children must align with cultural and religious norms. While non-Muslims have more flexibility in choosing names, there are still restrictions on using names from the 99 names of Almighty Allah."

Curious about the concept of Allah's names, I asked, "Is there a limit to these names?"

Quadria, Daria, Alara, and Hoda, all Muslims, chorused, "Yes. It is a part of our religion!" I marvelled at the knowledge that God's names in the Yoruba language were limitless. It reinforced my belief that the essence of God transcended any boundaries or limitations we humans might impose.

"Hey! Let me tell you something historical about the notorious Alaafin of the Oyo Empire, who forcefully crushed many West African towns. His exploit made the empire too large and vulnerable to incessant attacks from tributary towns that wanted independence," Ebun said, closing her book. She added playfully as all her friends began to listen to her with rapt attention, "You might want to sit up straight for this."

Ebun's classmates were intrigued by the historical practices she described and the examples she provided. They were particularly interested in the concept of the trusted war general and the idea of sacrificing one's life for loyalty and protection.

One of Ebun's classmates, Lisa, raised her hand and asked, "Ebun, I understand the importance of loyalty and sacrifice, but isn't it difficult to comprehend the idea of someone willingly dying alongside the king or offering their own life for another person?"

Ebun nodded and replied, "I understand your concern, Lisa. It is indeed a complex concept to grasp, especially from our modern perspective. However, we must remember that different cultures and historical periods had unique practices and beliefs. In the case of the Alaafin of Oyo Empire, the idea of the trusted war general sacrificing his life was a way to ensure the king's protection and the establishment of a strong bond of loyalty."

Chinedu, another classmate, chimed in, "But why would the general agree to such an arrangement? Wouldn't it be seen as an extreme measure?"

Ebun responded, "That's a valid question, Chinedu. The covenant between the Alaafin and the trusted war general was based on the belief that the general's sacrifice would guarantee the safety and longevity of the king's reign. It was a way to solidify their commitment and devotion. This practice was prevalent in Oyo until 1946 when it was officially abolished."

To further illustrate the concept of loyalty and sacrifice, Ebun shared the story of Lieutenant Colonel Adekunle Fajuyi, the first Military Governor of Western Nigeria. She recounted how Fajuyi selflessly sacrificed his life to protect the Head of State during a coup that also claimed his own life.

"There was a remarkable lieutenant colonel named Adekunle Fajuyi. He was the first military governor of Western Nigeria. On July 29, 1966, when Nigeria was engulfed in its second counter-coup and the nation was in turmoil, a group of armed mutineers sought to settle ethnic scores in a brutal and bloody manner. They stormed the government house in Ibadan, the capital of the old Western Region, and targeted the head of state, General Aguiyi Ironsi. The general happened to be on a visit to the governor at the time.

"They intended to kidnap and kill the head of state in revenge for the multiple murders committed by the plotters of Nigeria's first coup," Ebun paused to watch her classmates who were listening to her story with wide eyes.

"Then what happened?" Hoda asked.

Ebun continued, "In the chaos that ensued, a true gentleman officer emerged in the person of Adekunle Fajuyi. How could he stand idly by while his esteemed guest, his Supreme Commander, was being taken away to be killed under his roof?

"Adekunle Fajuyi refused to allow it to happen. He knew that if he succumbed to the mutineers' demands, it would only cause suspicion and that would perpetuate everlasting hatred woven into conspiracy theories. People would accuse the governor, who was not of the same tribe as the General, of betrayal and involvement in his death.

"With incredible bravery, Adekunle Fajuyi leapt onto the open Land Rover that was carrying the captured General. He made a selfless sacrifice for the sake of peace and unity in Nigeria. It was an act of loyalty to his boss, a display of gallantry that would leave the jaw of a medieval knight hanging slack in awe."

Ebun paused for a moment and reflected on the story she had just shared with her classmates. She couldn't help but draw a parallel to her ancestors, who also exhibited unwavering loyalty and made great sacrifices to protect their leaders. She decided that Governor Adeunle Fajuyi died for God, considering how he died, just like her ancestors did when protecting their leaders.

Ebun continued, "Adekunle Fajuyi's sacrifice of his life for General Aguiyi Ironsi reflects the same spirit of loyalty and protection that my ancestors displayed. Fajuyi's refusal to let harm come to his guest and commander, even at the risk of his life, demonstrates the depth of his commitment to peace and unity."

"OK, so those were different times you'd scoff, but let me give you an example from another time in history."

Ebun then referenced the biblical story of Lot from the good book of Genesis 19: 1-11 to further emphasise the theme of protection and sacrifice.

"So, one day in Sodom where Lot resided, two angels visited Sodom. Lot, recognising their divine nature, rose to meet them and bowed himself with his face toward the ground to show them reverence. The people of Sodom were not as welcoming or kind-hearted. They approached Lot's house and called out to him, demanding that he bring out the men whom he lodged in his home so that they could have their way with them. The intentions of the Sodomites were wicked and immoral.

"Lot went out to meet the mob, shutting the door behind him to protect the angels inside. He addressed the crowd and pleaded with them not to commit such atrocity. Lot even went to the extreme of offering his two daughters, who were virgins, as a substitute. He told them to do whatever they wanted with his daughters, but never to harm the angelic visitors as they had sought refuge under his roof."

Ebun took a deep breath and continued, "Despite the unrighteousness and depravity around him, he stood firm in his commitment to protect his guests. Lot's actions reflected his sense of responsibility and hospitality, as well as his willingness to make personal sacrifices to safeguard those in need.

"Just as the honourable Governor Adekunle Fajuyi demonstrated great loyalty and bravery in protecting his boss, Lot showed a similar sense of duty in safeguarding the divine messengers. These stories remind us of the importance of integrity, compassion, and standing up for what is right, even in the face of challenging circumstances."

At this point, some classmates raised concerns about the appropriateness of Lot's actions. Ebun acknowledged their concerns and said, "It's important to remember that the story of Lot is an ancient account that reflects the customs and values of that time. While we may view Lot's actions differently today, we must approach these stories with an understanding of the cultural context in which they were written.

"The examples I've shared are meant to illustrate the complexities of loyalty and sacrifice in different historical and cultural settings. They encourage us to reflect on the values that guided people's actions in those times even though we find them challenging now and can't relate with them."

Ebun's classmates listened attentively, their curiosity piqued by the intricate connections between history, culture, and the concepts of loyalty and sacrifice. They realised that exploring these ideas requires open-mindedness and a willingness to delve into the depths of different perspectives and contexts.

Among the students, Julia was listening quietly, with a question bubbling in her. After Ebun was done, Julia turned to the triplets and asked them, "Hey, your mother is from Offa, right? What is Ijakadi?"

The triplet's eyes lit up like candles, eager to showcase their cultural heritage to their classmates. The classroom buzzed with excitement as Ebun shared the details of the Ijakadi annual festival celebration in Offa, Kwara State.

"Oh, Ijakadi? It is a week-long festival with various activities starting with a press conference. Then follows juma'at service, church service, commissioning of projects, presentation of awards, traditional dances, parades by districts, wrestling bouts, and horse racing, among others. These activities are created to foster the bond of the people of the ancient town,"

Ebun explained enthusiastically.

Ife and I listened attentively, ready to contribute our knowledge to the discussion. Ebun took a deep breath, looked at Ife and asked, "Would you mind telling them the story, Ife?"

Ife smiled and nodded, stepping forward to address her curious classmates.

"Sure thing! The festival is rooted in a 14th-century account of two brothers who had a wrestling match at a river bank. It all started because they had lost a tuber of yam on their way back home from the farm," Ife began, capturing everyone's attention. "The incident resulted in a scuffle and argument about who should bear the pain of the lost yam. The king had to intervene and act as arbiter for a fair resolution. In the end, the king decided to share the remaining yams equally, giving each brother two and a half tubers of yam," Ife continued excitedly.

"The act of sharing things equally became a defining characteristic of the Offa people. It symbolises justice and equity embedded in the spirit of sharing. That's why the line from the epigrammatic panegyric of Offa reads, 'Ijakadi l'oro Offa', meaning wrestling is the custom or ritual of the Offa people," Ife explained.

As she finished recounting the story, the friends of the triplets were captivated by the historical account of the annual festival. Their mother's teachings had paid off, as the triplets confidently shared their cultural heritage with pride and authenticity. The classroom buzzed with discussions, and their classmates appreciated them for exposing them to the rich traditions of Offa. Julia, intrigued by the discussion, posed a question to the triplets. "Is the wrestling an exaggeration of a real performance or staged entertainment?" he asked.

Before the triplets could respond, Jessica interjected, "Yes, that's a good question because, in the world of sports, wrestling stands out. More than any other sport, wrestling blurs the line between athleticism and Hollywood entertainment and has profoundly impacted pop culture."

Quadria, eager to provide an answer, chimed in. "Everyone knows that professional wrestling matches are not legitimate contests. They are more like choreographed performances. Professional wrestlers are athletes playing characters and following storylines for an audience. However, more work goes into this industry than we know."

Curious, Hoda asked, "More work goes into it? How?"

Stacy, stepping forward to explain, replied, "Professional wrestlers must be aware of their abilities and limitations and keep themselves in a healthy physical state to perform at their optimum levels. They must know how to safely execute wrestling moves and always keep their opponents and themselves safe."

Fen, still puzzled, asked further. "So, the wrestling we watch is fake?"

Stacy clarified, "Wrestling is scripted, not fake. The outcome of matches is decided in advance. The promos are usually written and rehearsed before the show, and certain big moves you see throughout the matches are planned out and rehearsed beforehand to make them as safe as possible. Hardly will you see wrestlers full-on punching each other in the face.

"The athleticism from some of the more highflyers is never exaggerated, though. There are fan favourites whose fights are high-paced, and they constantly risk their safety to do something cool. Some wrestlers have developed a reputation for

jumping off something, usually a ladder, from a great height just to make the crowd react in fear. Wrestlers perform these types of stunts weekly to provide entertainment." Listening intently, Ebun interjected, "Well, I know that there's a world of difference between Western professional wrestlers and the wrestling that occurs at the festival in our mum's town. We haven't gone to witness it, but from what I've heard, the wrestlers don't throw punches at each other. They focus on grappling, striking, locking, and throwing techniques, just to ensure that the opponent's back touches the ground. The wrestlers don't need to use drugs of any kind or have superhuman bodies via steroids and other performance-enhancing drugs like Western wrestlers."

Antonella, curious about another topic, asked, "What about the world's most popular weed?"

Confused, some of the classmates asked, "What's the world's most popular weed?"

Julia quickly responded, "The world's most popular weed is marijuana, also known as cannabis and ganja."

Ebun, joining the conversation, added, "Oh, I didn't know it's the world's most popular weed. It's illegal to use cannabis, marijuana, or whatever names it's called. Why?"

Anima chimed in, "Cannabis is being decriminalised in some parts of the world."

Ebun shared our father's perspective when she said, "I heard my father say that Nigeria's stance on the criminalisation of cannabis users is due to crucial distinctions in the types of cannabis cultivated worldwide and the measures and quality standards those countries implemented. There are different species of cannabis, and those countries have better policies, enforcement, and measurement standards that people must follow. The decriminalised species in countries like the US, Canada, UK, Australia, Europe, and Caribbean countries lack Tetrahydrocannabinol (THC), the psychoactive component responsible for altering one's state of mind.

"In contrast, Nigerians cultivate cannabis strains with significantly higher potency, containing THC levels ranging from almost 45 percent to 100 percent. This makes them incomparable to the decriminalised variants." Intrigued, some classmates commented, "That's interesting!"

Ebun added, "The species they have, which they decriminalised in those countries, are those without Tetrahydrocannabinol, which is the active ingredient that can make one 'go gaga' or alter one's mind. Cannabinol, a constituent used in specific medical treatments, was previously permitted for importation, but restrictions have been imposed due to the increasing cannabinol content detected in the oil."

Stacy, still wanting to engage in the conversation, asked, "Is there any group exempted or allowed to use marijuana in Nigeria, like people of the Rastafari religion or faith because they consider marijuana as the 'holy weed' or herb? It's believed to induce a meditative state and bring them closer to the divine. The faithful smoke it as a sacrament and place it in fire as a burnt offering. Are they permitted?"

Ebun responded honestly, "I don't know. I will ask my father."

"Rastafarians, along with some Native Americans, do not use cannabis as a fun or party drug. For them, cannabis aids meditation and helps them to gain wisdom. They also use it as a sacrament," Stacy added.

Ebun, who was lost in thought, suddenly recalled something. Eager to share it, she began, "Another story my father, General Akin Olokun-Esin, told me about cannabis just crossed my mind. In 1992, the legendary Nigerian Afrobeat music pioneer Fela Anikulapo Kuti and the renowned Reggae musician Shabba Ranks had a cannabis smoking contest at the former's shrine.

"Shabba Ranks, born Ruxton Ralston Fernando Gordon on 17 January 1966, was one of the most popular Jamaican musicians in the late 1980s and early 1990s. Fela Anikulapo, born Olufela

Olusegun Ransome Kuti on 15 October 1938 and died on 2 August 1997, was a Nigerian musician, bandleader, composer, political activist and Pan-Africanist.

"In 1992, Shabba Ranks came to Nigeria to perform at a concert but decided to visit the Afrobeat legend at his Kalakuta shrine early in the day. Of course, he was blunt about the aim of his visit. Due to youthful exuberance, he told the legendary Afrobeat musician that he had heard about Fela's smoking legend and had come to claim the bragging rights for being the guy who out-smoked the Afrobeat pioneer."

Ebun paused for effect.

"Well, there's a saying that it is not wise to embark on a drinking or smoking challenge with another man if you do not underestimate your opponent," she said. "The legend, Fela, accepted the challenge, and the weed kings puffed away at their smokes while exchanging banter.

"Turns out, with each successful wrap of blunts, the rolls got bigger and bigger until Shabba Ranks eventually passed out. Apparently, he was heavily defeated because when he woke up, he was informed that he had missed his concert the previous night. The crowd, which had paid to watch him play his signature song 'Mr Loverman,' released the same year, 1992, was disappointed."

Ebun concluded the story, tying it back to the discussion, with a hint of caution in her voice. "Shabba Ranks got into trouble due to his ignorance of how different Nigeria's cannabis species is and his ill-advised attempt to out-smoke Fela. He lost a fortune when he missed his show."

The classroom fell into momentary silence as each student pondered the unexpected turn of events in the story. The triplets' classmates exchanged surprising looks as the consequences of underestimating the effects of cannabis dawned on them. The account left a strong impression on everyone present. They understood why it was important to use substances responsibly and know one's limits.

In our culturally diverse classroom, we revelled in the diversity of our names, traditions, and beliefs. It was a beautiful reminder that there are countless ways to honour and worship the divine, and our names were just one aspect of this vast tapestry of faith and culture. Our conversations about names, oriki, different cultures, and religions deepened our understanding of one another and nurtured a sense of respect and appreciation for our differences. It was a testament to the power of language, heritage, and the shared human experience that united us as classmates and friends.

After she finished narrating the event, Ebun sat at her desk, eagerly waiting for the lunch break to begin. She had been looking forward to playing with

Lisa and Ann outside and enjoying the warm sunshine. As the bell rang, signalling the start of the break, she hurriedly gathered her things and joined the bustling crowd of students making their way to the playground.

Amidst the laughter and chatter, Ebun noticed a girl from the class above hers walking towards their teacher, Mrs Johnson, with a worried expression. Curiosity piqued, Ebun hesitated for a moment before deciding to follow them; she wanted to know what was going on.

She stealthily approached the small group gathering around Mrs Johnson and strained her ears to catch snippets of their conversation. The girl, whose name was Tolu, spoke in a hushed voice. She was teary as she recounted her ordeal. It seemed that during the break, a boy from her class had kicked her in the stomach, causing her pain and discomfort.

Ebun's heart sank at the sight of Tolu's distress. She had never seen anyone hurt like this before, and she didn't know what to do. Mrs Johnson took charge immediately, her face etched with concern. She guided Tolu towards the sick bay, instructing another student to accompany them.

Ebun was full of confusion and worry as she watched them leave. She couldn't fathom why someone would intentionally hurt another person. She felt a knot in her stomach, a mixture of sympathy for Tolu and fear that something like this could happen to her or her friends.

Hours passed, and the school day was almost over. Mrs Johnson returned to the classroom with a solemn expression. She took a deep breath and addressed the class as she explained what had happened to Tolu. Ebun listened attentively as Mrs Johnson described how Tolu had experienced abdominal pain and started bleeding, which led to her being taken to the sick bay just as her parents were contacted.

Ebun's eyes widened with surprise and confusion. Blood? Why would Tolu be bleeding? With her voice filled with empathy and understanding, Mrs Johnson explained that the examination carried out at the clinic revealed that Tolu had just experienced her first menstrual flow, known as menarche. It turned out that this incident was not due to an act of violence but a medical condition called precocious puberty.

As Mrs Johnson delved into the topic, discussing the emotional and physical changes associated with early puberty, Ebun's initial shock transformed into a mix of curiosity and compassion. She realised that Tolu's body was maturing ahead of her emotional and cognitive development, which could be confusing and challenging for anyone her age.

The classroom fell silent as Mrs Johnson emphasised the importance of supporting Tolu and other children going through early puberty. She spoke about the heightened emotional changes they might experience and the need for understanding and empathy from their peers. Ebun became determined to be there for Tolu, to be her haven and support during this confusing time.

As the school day came to an end, Ebun found herself walking beside Tolu, offering a comforting smile and a reassuring presence. She listened as Tolu shared her worries and anxieties, and she assured her that she would be there whenever she needed someone to talk to. Ebun knew that being Tolu's friend meant being patient, understanding, and supportive.

That evening, Ebun shared the events of the day with her mother. She listened attentively; her face glowed with pride and admiration for her daughter's empathy and maturity. She reminded Ebun of the importance of understanding and accepting others, especially when they go through challenging times.

Ebun nodded, her heart filled with a renewed sense of compassion. She understood that early puberty could bring about feelings of isolation and confusion, and she was determined to be a positive force in Tolu's life. Consequently, Ebun resolved to be Tolu's coach, cheering squad, and steadfast friend. She promised to help her navigate the complexities of early puberty with love, affirmation, and support.

We all loved going to school and woke up effortlessly to the sound of our mum reciting poetry and the delicious aroma of breakfast in the air.

I woke up one day and saw that Ife was still sound asleep while Ebun was already up and downstairs. Ebun was holding a newspaper that our father had already read that morning. Her eyes went over every line, taking it one word at a time and absorbing everything she read. She was an avid reader, a habit she got from our father, General Olokun-Esin, who was very fond of reading himself. He loved us all dearly, but Ebun was his favourite. He was awarded a Nigerian Star for his conspicuous bravery, and he earned the respect of his family and friends. He was a man of strong nerves. He won many medals for his service in the army, and he was an exceptional leader. He was like the Alaafin of Oyo in many ways.

The Alaafin of Oyo was a highly respected traditional ruler who ruled over his people for many years. He was known for his wisdom, his ability to resolve disputes, and his deep knowledge of Yoruba culture and tradition. His people looked up to him as the symbol of their cultural heritage, and he was a unifying force for his kingdom. He was just like our father, who always went out of his way to help people and act as a unifying force, whether in the community or family.

Our father was a highly decorated military officer who served his country with distinction. He was known for his courage, tactical expertise, and his ability to lead his troops to victory in difficult situations. He was respected by his fellow officers and soldiers for his professionalism and dedication to duty.

Comparing the two, I would say that the Alaafin of Oyo and General Olokun-Esin both possessed certain qualities that made them strong leaders in their respective domains. While the Alaafin was a traditional ruler who represented the cultural heritage and values of his people, General Olokun-Esin was a military leader who represented the strength and resilience of his country's armed forces. Both leaders had to navigate complex challenges and make difficult life decisions to rise to glory to protect and serve their families and communities. The Alaafin maintained the cultural identity and traditions of his kingdom while ensuring the safety and prosperity of his people. Similarly, General Olokun-Esin defended our country and our family against internal and external threats while upholding the values of the military profession.

While the roles of the Alaafin of Oyo and General Olokun-Esin were vastly different, they shared some similarities in terms of leadership qualities and responsibilities. Both leaders were highly respected by their people and proved themselves to be strong and effective in their respective domains. People always told us how we demonstrate his qualities and we could not be prouder.

Our mum, Mrs Olokun-Esin, was sitting on a sofa with our father, and Ebun was sitting on a bean bag right next to the table where our father had put his laptop. Ebun continued to read an article that she started reading earlier. She kept reading it even though it was way too serious and boring for her age. Typical Ebun!

"Nigeria is plagued by weak governance and it is a strong barrier to quality healthcare delivery. It hinders productivity and effectiveness and negatively affects user satisfaction, the quality of infrastructure, and health outcomes. People in government and leadership positions are significantly tasked with improving healthcare services and systems. However, they keep failing miserably. As the most important stakeholder in the health sector, government must assume accountability at all levels. To prevent the collapse of basic healthcare, we must move rapidly."

My sister's interest grew and her smile faded as she continued to read. The article's content highlighted the fragile status of healthcare in Nigeria, where access to health services is hampered by systemic problems in every state. The article further reads:

"The public health facilities in all 36 states and the FCT are inadequate, and community members who seek medical attention at public institutions often have terrible experiences.

"In 13 states, the Basic Health Care Provision Fund (BHCPF) was not properly implemented.

"Primary healthcare is the hardest to get in Zamfara, Nigeria.

"Weak governance frameworks and operational inefficiencies are the root reasons for Nigeria's failing healthcare system.[1]

"Over the past 20 years, statistics about child mortality in Nigeria indicate that 115 children die before their fifth birthday.

"Respiratory, gastrointestinal, and infectious diseases—diseases that were previously recognised as substantial contributors to childhood mortality— are the leading causes of death among children under the age of five. Only if the government and donor organisations go outside the health sector to discover underlying causal elements such as education and housing and inside the health sector, such as robust maternity, neonatal, and child health programs, child mortality could be reduced by two-thirds.[2]"

I was helping Ife in the kitchen, but I saw that Ebun became teary as she read the awful statistics about the healthcare condition of her country. The statistics was true. The area of child healthcare has been neglected, hence, many children die before they reach the age where their immune systems get strong enough to fight for them.

My lovely sister Ebun was a young girl. She was only ten years old, but she was aware of what was happening around her. The credit mostly went to our father, who always gently answered her every question. His patient disposition built her interest in knowing more.

Ebun raised her head from the newspaper and looked at our father, who was busy working on his laptop, and our mother, who was sipping her morning

They were unaware of what Ebun was reading. My parents also hated how things were in Nigeria. However, they could not do anything about it except feel bad and try to give their little angels the best healthcare they could afford.

"Mum, Dad, will I be able to get an organ transplant if my body stops working?" Ebun asked with childish innocence. Mum was shocked at her question and asked her to sit with her. Ebun got up from her bean bag and walked up to her with the newspaper in her hand. Father picked her up and made her sit on his lap. It was her favourite place to sit when she wanted to ask all the silly and important questions to her heart's content and get all the answers she needed.

"My sunshine, why did you ask this question? And how do you know about organ transplants?" he asked with curiosity.

"I was reading this article that you were reading when I woke up, and I read that there is a shortage of organs and tissues for transplantation in Nigeria. Every year, many people and kids die because they cannot get proper medical attention and health services in Nigeria every year. I was wondering if I would be able to get an organ transplant and be healthy again if I get sick," Ebun said as she waved the newspaper in our father's face.

Mr and Mrs Olokun-Esin looked at their daughter and were impressed. It was only a few years ago when we celebrated her first baby steps, and now we were looking at her all grown up and asking critical questions.

"My angel, I will take care of you to the best of my abilities and will never let anything harm you," our father assured her, caressing her face with love. "I will get you the best healthcare and a better life, even if it means going somewhere else where you can be better-taken care of. Why do you think you will not get proper care here in Nigeria?"

Ebun ran her finger across the page. "Here! It says here that the development of medical technology has made it possible to extend the lives of organ-impaired people through organ transplantation. However, because the number of patients on the waiting list outnumbers the number of organs available, one of the main obstacles to organ transplantation in Nigeria is a shortage of organs. The writer of this article examines the current

problems and issues with organ donation and transplantation in Nigeria, including the sale of organs to the highest bidder, consent issues, compromised medical staff, cultural and religious influences, a lack of a strong legal system in Nigeria, and a shortage of cutting-edge medical equipment!"

She looked at her parents, who kept staring proudly at her and then continued, "In the last ten years, there has been a sharp rise in the demand for organ transplants in Nigeria due to growing vital organ failure rates. There are severe organ shortage emergencies because of insufficient organs and tissues for transplantation to match the current demand. Therefore, both the number of people dying while waiting for a transplant and the number of people on transplant waiting lists have significantly increased."

"Isn't it sad, Ebun? Some want to help others out by donating their organs but cannot do so even when they want to." Mother said as she put her glasses on the table.

"Why can't they? Who is stopping them, Mum?" Ebun asked in an angry tone.

Mum took a deep breath and answered, "Well, there are a couple of reasons they do not come forward. One of them is that they do not trust medical personnel to harvest their organs. This is because government-run public hospitals lack the necessary equipment for

the effective delivery of healthcare services. The fact that some commercial hospitals have better equipment than government-owned hospitals presents a problem. Rich people may pay more for better care in private hospitals, while a greater proportion of Nigerians live in poverty. Rich people may travel outside of Nigeria for organ surgeries because of these reasons, but the cost of proper healthcare, including organ donation and transplantation, is high and beyond the means of the average Nigerian family."

"That is so sad, Mum," Ebun interjected, "I wish people would donate their organs to save others and see it as an act of valour and compassion."

Mum was worried and asked, "But Ebun if someone is going to donate all their organs, how are they going to survive?"

Ebun was just a kid. She thought for a moment and then said, "They can donate their organs, but only if for some reason they die or fall terminally ill, because then they would not need them. We can save so many lives that way. So even if they are going to die, they can save so many people!"

Mum was stunned by her answer and hugged her tightly.

This conversation made our parents begin to think critically about the healthcare situation in the country. They could not help but think about our future. They were there for us, but they were also thinking about all the other kids who may not be privileged

enough to get proper healthcare if the government hospital nearest to them failed them.

According to a World Health Organization report, Nigeria has the fourth worst healthcare system in the world. We live in a nation without ambulance services or a straightforward toll-free number like 911 to contact in an emergency. The likelihood of surviving a heart attack is quite slim in Nigeria. Perhaps a little too severe but some individuals have said that hospitals in Nigeria are places where people go to die. Nigerians appear to have accepted the inevitability of early death if they were unfortunate enough to be diagnosed with any significant sickness because the public health system is plagued by a lack of medications, medical equipment, and medical professionals.

All humans yearn to use every means possible to prolong their lives because they believe that life is sacred. This is one desire that is at odds with what Nigeria offers her citizens with her dilapidated healthcare system. Organ transplantation is a viable method for replacing damaged human organs.

However, because of the numerous restrictions and difficulties associated with such transplants, this opportunity is not entirely accessible in Nigeria. With the donor's agreement and little danger to the patient in the waiting period, surgical treatments like organ transplantation will be ethically acceptable. Additionally, the genuine death of the donor must be conclusively established before this honourable act of organ donation may take place. But because of some people, organ transplants have become difficult and troublesome even when there are ready donors. These people are divided into three categories: first, the traffickers who would trick the victim into giving up his organ for free; second, the "con -artists" who would persuade innocent victims into selling their organs and then not pay them the agreed sum or not at all; and third, the doctors who treat their patients for non- existent ailments and diseases and, by extension, steal the patients' organs.

It is right to state that Nigeria has no laws governing organ donation and transplantation. It is also safe to argue that the country has the National Health Act of 2014, which has numerous flaws and does not fully address the practice as it now exists in our society.[3]

While many may strive to hasten the procedure, there are still laws that must be followed since more individuals are waiting for organ and tissue transplants than there are donors. Each year, hundreds of lives are saved thanks to the donation of organs and tissues, but these donations must go through the right procedures.

Another problem that has to be resolved is the absence of a national registry for organ donation or transplantation in the country. In Nigeria, neither the physicians nor the patients know what organ transplant legislation is. Every hospital simply uses its internal procedures.

For instance, receivers usually bring in commercial donors who pose as family members. Because of that, most hospitals in Nigeria require family members to donate organs to shield their staff and the hospital from lawsuits. They often require an affidavit from a court of law before they perform a transplant. This often leads to transplant tourism outside of Nigeria, even if

Organ transplantation raises important ethical, legal, and societal concerns that require extensive discussion. Many nations have implemented transplant legislation and restrictions on commercial organ trade, but transplant tourism continues to flourish in many regions of the world, including first-world nations. Due to the levels of poverty and corruption in developing countries like Nigeria, we need to do better to regulate transplant activities.

General Akin Olokun-Esin was in deep thought and distress after Ebun gave him an innocent reality check. On the other hand, Ebun spent her day thinking about the people who could not afford to get organs transplanted or the people who wanted to volunteer but were scared to trust medical personnel. She was fascinated by the whole process, and she felt sad for people who were waiting for their lives to be saved. She thought about people who would demand and expect monetary advantages for donating their organs.

Her conversation with our parents got her thinking, and she went to sleep with these thoughts in her head. However, Ife and I observed that she had a fitful sleep as she kept waking up intermittently, which was quite unusual for her. She later decided to learn more about the issue, but there was no way she could get more information. She, therefore, turned to the internet. She was as curious as a cat and desperately wanted to discuss the topic with her friends at school. She could not discuss it with us because we were always busy with our shenanigans and had little or no time to listen to her childish rants. She had a couple of friends who would find the topic interesting, so she closed her eyes and tried to sleep once again. Hardly could she wait to get to school the next day so she could share her concerns with her classmates.

CHAPTER 1 DISCUSSION QUESTIONS:

1. What are some key characteristics of Nigeria's cultural diversity that the author highlights in Chapter 1?

2. How does Nigeria's ability to embrace people from diverse ethnic backgrounds contribute to its strength and resilience as a nation?

3. In what ways do the three major ethnic groups in Nigeria (Hausa- Fulani, Yoruba, and Igbo) enrich the cultural fabric of the country?

4. How does the narrator's fourth-grade classroom reflect the cultural diversity of Nigeria? What did the author and their classmates learn from this diversity?

5. What did the author learn from Antonella's essay about naming conventions in Latin American countries? How does this relate to the theme of cultural diversity?

6. How did Pierre Fatumbi Verger's work and his connection to Nigeria's culture impact the author and their classmates? Why is it significant?

7. Why is preserving and embracing one's native language, as demonstrated by the author and their sisters, important in understanding and connecting with one's culture?

CHAPTER 2

AANU

I t was a fine Monday morning in Abuja, and Ebun had just opened her eyes. As she woke up, she told me that her first thought was about the article she read the day before. All the statistics and facts were imprinted in her memory, and she felt sad for all the people who were not privileged enough to get an organ transplant or proper health care. Nigeria is filled with stories of people dying due to improper health care conditions. Ebun did not have to worry about it, though, since ours was an upper-class family, but she knew that not everyone around her was as fortunate, and that made her feel miserable. She was excited to discuss and share her views with her friends at school, so she jumped out of bed and started getting ready for school.

She woke up without our mum's prompt. Unlike other kids, Ebun liked going to school. She was a good student and had a huge circle of friends. Due to her curiosity, all her teachers were very fond of her. She was innocent and eager to learn and create. Our parents were proud of her, and they cared for all her needs.

The minute she came out of the bathroom, she put the newspaper with the troubling article in her school bag. When she came downstairs, our parents were already up and busy reading the newspaper as usual.

"Good morning, Sunshine. Did you have a good night's sleep?" Mum asked Ebun as she hugged her. Ife made a face to express her displeasure at the undue attention Ebun was receiving.

"Good morning, Mum. I had a great sleep and had no nightmares," Ebun said innocently as she sat next to her Mum kissed her on the cheeks before responding to her. Ife and I came out of the kitchen, smiling as we held our trays with our delicious breakfast and the orange juice Mum had prepared for us, which Ebun loved. We then began to eat our healthy and nutritious breakfast. Although Ebun received special affection from all of us, she was not a spoiled brat, and neither were we. Also, she didn't abuse the special attention she got. She was aware and grateful for the life that she lived and very respectful of our parents. When we finished eating our breakfast, we picked up our bags and went to the car, where our driver was waiting to take us to school.

"You are going to be late, Miss Ebun," our driver said teasingly like he does every day.

Ebun smiled at him and said, "Have faith, old man." That was her usual response to him every morning.

We set off to school while listening to music and chit-chatting in the car. We saw other kids also going to school. Others were not so privileged to attend a school; they could only help their parents with work. Some were out already and selling different items in traffic. Our school was one of the best in Abuja. We attended an American international school; most of the students belonged to the upper class of society.

As the car pulled up in front of the school gates, I glanced nervously at my sisters, Ife and Ebun, who sat next to me in the backseat. We were all dressed in our school uniforms, crisp white blouses and green skirts, with our hair neatly tied back in matching ribbons. It was the first day of the new term, and we were all feeling a little bit apprehensive.

The driver opened the door, and I stepped out onto the pavement and took a deep breath. The air was hot and humid, with the sun already beating down on us. I turned to help Ife out of the car and then watched as Ebun climbed out behind us.

We walked toward the school building. As we made our way through the school gate and toward our classroom, I felt a rush of excitement mixed with nerves. I knew we were going to have a great day though; I was also sure we were going to make lots of new friends.

"Come on," I said, taking their hands. "Let's go show them what we're made of!"

It was harmattan season, and everyone was wearing warm clothes. The school was filled with students running around and playing pranks on each other. It was Monday, so everyone had stories from their weekend to tell. There was a lot of buzz throughout the school.

We got into our class, where our friends were already settling down. Ebun sat down at her desk, which was right in front of the teacher's desk. She sat with her best friend, Lisa.

Ebun and Lisa were both ten years old and had been inseparable since they met in their first year of school. They shared a love for learning and spent most of their time together studying and exploring new subjects.

Lisa was an intelligent and curious student who always asked questions and was never afraid to speak her mind. She had a contagious enthusiasm for learning that inspired her friends and teachers. Her favourite subjects were mathematics and science, and she dreamed of becoming an engineer someday.

By contrast, Ebun was more reserved and introspective, but she was just as passionate about her studies as Lisa. She was a talented writer and enjoyed reading books about history and culture. She hoped to become a journalist someday and use her writing skills to make a difference in her community.

Despite their different personalities and interests, Ebun and Lisa complemented each other perfectly. They often worked together on school projects and assignments, and their combined knowledge and creativity always produced outstanding results.

Outside of school, Ebun and Lisa enjoyed playing games and exploring their neighbourhood. They often visited the local library, where they read books and learned about different cultures and countries. They also enjoyed playing soccer and other sports with their classmates.Their friendship was so strong that they were often called "two peas in a pod" by their classmates. They supported each other through the ups and downs of school and life, and their bond only grew stronger with each passing day.

Ebun and Lisa were two exceptional students who shared a deep friendship and a love for learning. Also, they brought out the best in each other. Their friendship was an inspiration to everyone around them.

After their English class was over and their English teacher left, Anele, a South African student of mixed race, excused herself. She said she needed to use the restroom. Little did she know that her movement would lead to a rather amusing and enlightening moment.

As Anele left the classroom, a peculiar scent filled the air, catching the attention of two mischievous classmates, including Anima, who was from India. They quickly pointed at Anele and decided that she was responsible for the unpleasant odour. Anima couldn't resist adding a remark, "That half- caste must have polluted the atmosphere."

Ebun, known for her strong sense of fairness and respect, immediately spoke up in protest. She firmly insisted, "Anima! Stop referring to her as a half-caste. It is outdated at best but more importantly offensive. Calling anyone 'half ' of something is dehumanising and derogatory. If we consider ourselves half, does that mean everyone else is whole? And when those of us with mixed heritage have children, what will they be labelled? Shouldn't we move beyond such fractional terms?"

Her words hung in the air, causing a momentary silence in the classroom. Curiosity sparked among her classmates as they pondered the implications of Ebun's perspective. It was clear that her words had struck a chord, and they were eager to delve deeper into the topic.

Taking advantage of the moment, Ebun decided to shed light on the word "caste" and its various meanings. She explained that while they might be familiar with the caste system in India, which had perpetuated segregation and negativity for centuries, the term "half-caste" has a different origin. It originated from the Latin word "Castus," meaning pure, and its Spanish and Portuguese derivative, "caste," which implies impurity. The term implies that only white heritage is pure while any other heritage muddles the bloodline. Ebun found this idea inherently wrong.

Anima listened attentively, her expressions changing from surprise to contemplation. It was a profound moment as the students questioned the usage of derogatory terms, preferring to embrace inclusivity and respect for all regardless of diverse backgrounds.

After lecturing her classmates on race relations, she went to the cafeteria with Lisa.

"Lisa, do you know about this? There's a massive shortage of organ donors and facilities throughout Nigeria?" Ebun said, showing her the newspaper article.

"People trick others into removing their organs? That is sick!" Lisa said in disgust.

Lisa, Ebun's best friend, became immediately interested in the subject and sat beside her friend to read the article. Lisa belonged to a wealthy family; her father was an executive in an American oil company.

"That is not even the worst part," Ebun said, raising her eyebrows. "Sometimes, people agree to give their organs for money and they end up not being compensated for it."

"That is horrible. So many kids die due to this," Ann said as she joined them at the table. Ann was one of Ebun's classmates and a dear friend.

Although Ebun and Lisa were the best of friends, Ann was their fellow friend and she was quite different from them. Ann was an introvert and didn't speak much. She was always lost in thought and didn't seem to enjoy the same things that Ebun and Lisa enjoyed. While Ebun and Lisa loved going out and having fun, Ann preferred to stay at home and read books.

Ann was also very independent; she didn't rely on anyone for anything and preferred to do things her way. That was unlike Ebun and Lisa, who always relied on each other for support.Despite their differences, Ebun and Lisa loved Ann and appreciated her unique personality. They understood that everyone can't be the same and that's what made their friendship so special. They respected Ann's independence and her love for reading and often asked her for book recommendations.

Ann, in turn, appreciated Ebun and Lisa's outgoing personalities and their willingness to try new things. She admired their confidence and their ability to make friends easily. She often wished she could be more like them but she knew that wasn't who she was.

In the end, their differences didn't matter. They remained best of friends and always would be. They learned from each other and grew together, even if they didn't always understand each other's perspectives. Their relationship was a testament to the power of true friendship and the beauty of diversity.

"You know about this?" Ebun said.

"Yes, and you know what? Spain is one of the leading countries in organ transplants in the world. Spain has been the world's leader in organ donation and transplantation for 27 straight years," Ann said while taking a look at the article.

It was true that Spain demonstrated its ability to constantly improve in 2018 by reaching 48 donors per million population (p.m.p.), a total of 2,243 donors, enabling 5,314 organs to be transplanted. These values indicated six donors and 14.6 organ transplants every day, according to the Spanish National Transplant Organization (ONT).

Mara Luisa Carcedo, Minister of Health, Consumption, and Social Well-being reiterated these results at a news conference, where she also presented the ONT's activity data for 2018. The minister was accompanied by the secretary-general for health,

Faustino Blanco, and Beatriz Dominguez-Gil, the director of the Spanish National Transplant Organization."That is impressive! I wish Nigeria could do that. We would be able to save so many lives," Lisa said as she made a sad face. She then added, "Nigerian children have a terrible transplant access rate of 0.2%. The main problem is a lack of finance. The government must support healthcare, particularly kidney transplants, immediately."

"Hey, do not worry, you guys; it is just a matter of educating people. The future is bright, and we are brighter," Ebun said, putting her arm over Lisa's shoulder.

"Aw, thank you, Ebun. That is why you are my best friend," Lisa said, chuckling.

"Educating people and raising awareness! That is a fantastic idea, don't you guys think?" Ann said like a light bulb just got turned on in her head.

"What do you mean?" Ebun asked innocently.

Ann explained, "If all of us took care of each other. If all of us had two best friends, we could raise awareness and start a chain reaction. That way, we will always have donors and the success rate for organ transplants will rise. This should be a national movement."

"Sometimes, I wish they would make you the president. That would be great," Lisa said while drinking her chocolate milk.

"Yeah, we will not have to go to school or take exams if Ann is president," said Ebun as she laughed.

"Jokes aside, there was an incident involving one of my neighbours regarding his kidney transplant," Ebun said, and her friends immediately stopped whatever they were doing to listen to her.

Ebun continued, "A neighbour's son fell seriously ill and it was diagnosed to be kidney failure. In the family's hopelessness, a relative came to their rescue and informed them that there was someone who could help them. They arranged to fly them to India to get the procedure done since it couldn't be done here in Nigeria."

"How is he now?" Lisa asked with concern.

Ebun looked at both faces and then said, "He did not make it!"

Both friends gasped, and then Ebun continued, "Turns out that the guy who went with them scammed them and ran away with $20,000. They returned home after being scammed, and the sick boy died after three weeks."

"That is awful. Why would people do that? Why are these offenders not jailed?" Ann asked in anger.

"That is the issue. There are no proper laws and regulations regarding that. There should be a law about organ transplants to stop trafficking and scamming," Ebun said.

A new and major component of the burgeoning healthcare sector has been the migration of patients across borders in search of medical treatment and healthcare, a phenomenon known as medical tourism. This medical phenomenon includes a whole range of medical services. However, surgical operations, including organ transplants, are among the most common treatments patients receive from other countries.

This trend in the movement of patients and, on occasion, medical workers across borders has provided relief to those who could not previously get medical treatment. Thus, transplant (organ) tourism comprises the cross-border movement of organs, donors, or patients. Transplant tourism may be classified into four types:

1. The recipient travels to the nation where the transplant centre and donor are situated.

2. The donor travels to the nation of the recipient and transplant centre.

3. The donor and recipient go together to the nation where the transplant centre is located.

4. The donor and recipient travel from separate nations to the transplant centre

in another country.

Transplant tourism has been recorded in several countries, with destinations including India, Pakistan, the Philippines, Egypt, China, and Mexico, among others. However, there is no clear data on the prevalence of transplant tourism/organ trafficking in these countries. Organ trafficking is estimated to account for 5-10% of all kidney transplants performed globally each year.

In Nigeria, there is a rising number of patients with kidney transplant cases and transplant centres. Meanwhile, only two of the eight centres that have done kidney transplants are regularly transferring. A report from Nigeria's most active transplant centre, presented by Ebun Bamgboye at the biennial satellite symposium of the World Congress of Nephrology (10th conference on kidney disease in disadvantaged populations) in Cape Town, South Africa, in 2015, revealed that more than half of their kidney transplant population received their transplant from abroad.[5]

The bell rang, and it was time for them to go for their next session. They finished their meal hurriedly while still discussing the topic Ebun had chosen to discuss that day. The trio were young, but they were aware of the critical problems in their society that needed to be addressed to save precious lives.

CHAPTER 2 DISCUSSION QUESTIONS:

1. How did Ebun feel about the article on organ transplants and healthcare in Nigeria, and why did it affect her so deeply?

2. What are the characteristics of Ebun, Ife, and Ann, and how do their personalities complement each other in their friendship?

3. What important lessons did Ebun share with her classmates about the use of derogatory terms and the need for inclusivity and respect for diverse backgrounds?

4. How did the conversation about organ transplants lead to a discussion of medical tourism and organ trafficking, and what are the key challenges faced by patients in Nigeria regarding organ transplants?

5. What potential solutions did Ebun, Lisa, and Ann discuss to address the challenges in organ transplantation and raise awareness about the issue in Nigeria?

CHAPTER 3

AANU

We lived in Abuja, Nigeria's capital city. Abuja is pleasant. It was dusty and dry throughout the Harmattan season, Africa's version of winter. However, with the rainy season or summer showers, the weather got cooler. Abuja is a very friendly city. The people are kind and polite, and life is not as fast-paced as it is in Lagos. Many working Nigerians made less than USD$200-300 a month. A great number of people managed significantly less.

As for me, Ife, and Ebun, we lived with our parents. Our mum was a housewife who loved her family greatly. She got married at a young age and stayed at home. Our father, Olokun-Esin, on the other hand, was a general. He was a man of vigour, solid principles, and discipline. His military background was the reason we lived a luxurious and harmonious life.

We lived in the upscale neighbourhood of Asokoro on Hassan Katsina Street where all the elites of the city resided. Hassan Katsina Street in Asokoro, Abuja, is a truly exquisite neighbourhood with houses that boast stunning architecture, elegant

landscaping, and an alluring ambience that captivates anyone who sets foot on its paved streets.

As one stroll down the tree-lined avenues of Hassan Katsina Street, one is welcomed by grandiose mansions and luxurious villas that exude opulence and sophistication in every detail. The stunning facades of these magnificent homes are adorned with intricate designs, beautiful balconies, and grand entrances befitting only royalty.

The lush greenery that surrounds these stately homes is impeccably maintained, with manicured lawns and vibrant flower beds that add a touch of natural beauty to this urban oasis. The well-paved roads are lined with streetlights that make the neighbourhood glow with warmth and welcoming vibes even at night.

Exploring Hassan Katsina Street further, one would notice the air is filled with the sounds of laughter and joyful chatter. The residents of this neighbourhood are friendly and welcoming. They create a sense of community that is truly heartwarming.

Overall, Hassan Katsina Street is a haven of elegance and luxury that offers a unique blend of natural beauty and modern sophistication. It is truly a gem of a neighbourhood that anyone would be lucky to call home.

Our family had a villa that had a backyard dotted with lots of flowers and plants. Everyone in our house had an air-conditioned room.

We owned a car, and we were never short of anything because our family was pretty well-off.

As triplets, we shared a unique bond. We took care of and loved one another, dearly. Apart from the occasional sibling arguments, we were known to be very well-behaved and civilised. We looked after one another and shared everything like the best of friends. We were far ahead of our age as 10-year- old middle school kids.

"What are you doing there, Ebun?" I asked her as she scrolled through her phone.

"I am drawing our family. See, this is you, and that is Ife. Here's Dad, and here is Mum," Ebun said as she showed me the drawing she had made on her iPad.

"That looks great, Ebun, but where are you in this?" I asked.

"I am going to draw myself in the end. I also want my hair to be longer, so I might draw myself after a month when my hair gets longer," Ebun said with childish innocence. Ife and I exchanged glances. Then, Ife, who was busy having her favourite brand of chocolate, joined the conversation.

"Hey, Ebun, what are you going to do when you are all grown up? she asked without taking her eyes off the chocolate bar she was far from finishing.

"Well, when I grow up, I am going to be just like Dad. I am going to help people in faraway places and fight for my country," Ebun said.

"But who are you going to fight? We are not facing any enemies or threats," I asked.

"I don't necessarily have to fight with people. I want to fight hunger and diseases," Ebun said while drawing buttons on our father's uniform.

We were shocked at her answer. I came closer and sat beside her and said to her, "That is great! Where did you get this inspiration?"

"I read it in the newspaper." Ebun took out the piece of paper she kept folded in the front pocket of her pink hoodie and placed it in front of me. "It says here that one out of every ten kids in Nigeria dies because of improper healthcare. When there is an organ transplant situation, the chances of the kids' survival drop drastically. If this is not a threat, then what is it? Hunger and bad healthcare situations are the enemy, and we should fight them before it is too late. What if there is a disease outbreak like a plague or something? If we do not have enough resources to take care of existing problems, then how are we going to take care of anything unforeseen?"

We smiled as she finished her little exposition with a question.

We saw that the article that Ebun had read deeply influenced and touched her heart. She was genuinely worried about the healthcare situation and felt guilty that she enjoyed immense benefits as a major general's daughter, a benefit that most kids in her country could not enjoy or afford or did not even know existed.

Since the day she read the article, Ebun felt the urge to talk to everyone about the topic. Whether she was at home, at school, or playing with her friends, it was the only thing that she talked about. She was researching with what resources she had, and she told everyone about the problem; it was fast becoming her obsession. She was already performing the duties of an activist without knowing it.

As she researched and discussed the topic, she became more aware of how deep the problem was. Children indeed have access to unlimited information and resources through the internet, so they do not need tutors as long as they are interested in anything.

After diving deep into a *YouTube* rabbit hole, Ebun discovered that one of the greatest obstacles in Nigeria's healthcare system is the ignorance of individuals about their present health problems. Patients were not enlightened to learn about their health condition. They were not actively engaged in the decision-making process that concerns improving their well-being, since most Nigerians rely largely on medical advice from untrained persons such as family members.

Furthermore, due to a lack of clarity about the ailments residents experience, many patients are misdiagnosed. This phenomenon is common with institutions with insufficiently educated staff. Misdiagnoses are particularly widespread in Nigeria because there is minimal investment in the workforce. As a result, many Nigerians don't seek medical advice from doctors until their ill health drastically worsens.

One of the key issues in Nigeria's healthcare business is the insufficient allocation of financial resources to enhance and sustain the health of the general population. The distribution of healthcare resources is lopsided, with a large amount going to secondary and tertiary care facilities. This means that individuals are bound to avoid basic healthcare in favour of better care in secondary and tertiary facilities.

This inevitably leads to inefficiencies since these facilities are overcrowded with medical concerns that may be treated at the basic level. Meanwhile, care is more expensive at secondary and tertiary care centres, where average

Nigerians are usually unable to afford the cost of this care.

The more Ebun learned about these statistics and figures, the more she got worried. Our mum saw that her daughter was worried and working on something worth worrying about; she could not be prouder. She discussed it with Ebun and told her that she was very

happy with her and that she got this sense of responsibility from her father.

"Girls! Dinner is ready." Mum stood at the foot of the stairs and looked up as she called to us. Ebun was already downstairs at the dinner table with our parents while Ife and I came down to join them. After we were all seated, our father's batmen came with our meal. We were about to have a meal of *suya* and jollof rice, culinary delicacies in Nigeria.

"*Suya!* Thanks, Mum," Ebun exclaimed and started on the kebab placed in front of her. *Suya* was her favourite dish. While we ate, Ebun started a discussion with our father about her newest obsession: healthcare.

Our father's job as a military man is a tough one, but he always found time to talk to Ebun as if they were age-mates. Whenever she engaged him in conversations and asked him a million questions, he would indulge her and answer all her questions very calmly and politely. We all were achievers for this reason, as we never hesitated to ask questions.

Ebun and Father's discussion went on till after dinner, and when she was satisfied, she kissed him goodnight, folded the small piece of paper she carried around and put it in her pocket. When she lay in bed, she kept thinking about solutions to her country's problems. She slept with the article close to her chest.

CHAPTER 3 DISCUSSION QUESTIONS:

1. How would you describe the family's living situation and neighbourhood in Abuja? What does their lifestyle reveal about their social and economic status?

2. What aspirations does Ebun have, and how is her family's background influencing her goals?

3. How did Ebun's encounter with the newspaper article about healthcare issues affect her? Why did she become so passionate about addressing these problems?

4. What were some of the key healthcare challenges and issues in Nigeria discussed by Ebun as she delved deeper into the topic? How were these issues affecting the general population?

5. How is Ebun's father supportive of her interests and questions, and how does this influence the children's inquisitive nature and pursuit of knowledge?

CHAPTER 4

AANU

E bun knew this place. She had spent a lot of time playing on these streets with her friends from the adjoining neighbourhoods. But this street did not look the same. People were running frantically. There was panic and hysteria. She did not know what was happening.

"I can't breathe! I can't breathe…" A man in his mid-50s limped towards her with his son following him. His son was about the same age as Ebun. Ambulances began to rush to an unknown destination. Some ambulances were parked in front of different houses. Kids were screaming, and their mothers were crying and pleading with people in hazmat suits to help them. Chaos had engulfed the area. Ebun was panicky; she looked for her family, but she couldn't find anyone.

As she walked towards her house, she saw two people fighting over an oxygen tank. The two tall men were aggressively pulling at the oxygen tank, pleading and swearing for its possession. For some reason, people were wearing face masks. She had not seen people wear masks like that. She did not know what was wrong, but she knew that something was not right and the situation was out of control. She walked until she got home. The door was open, so she walked inside, but there was no one there. Her siblings' rooms were empty, and her father's Batman was also nowhere to be found.

"Get out of the house, Ebun." Ebun heard a stern worried voice call her name. She recognised her mother's voice and followed it to own parents' bedroom.

The room's door was closed and sealed with yellow police tapes. Throwing all caution to the wind, she ripped the tape off and opened the door. What she saw sent shudders down her spine.

Mum was lying on her bed with Dad sitting on a chair nearby. His head was resting on the headrest of the chair and his eyes rolled back. Mum looked skinnier, and her voice was hoarse. She was coughing badly. As Ebun came closer, her mum gestured to her to stay away. Her hand was covered in blood. Ebun was scared. She took two steps back and felt someone behind her. Before she could turn, she felt two glove-clad hands grab her by her shoulders. Ebun tried to scream, but she could not. As she writhed to get free, she woke up.

She was still in bed, sweating profusely. It was a nightmare. She was panting and crying, overwhelmed with fear and loneliness. Fortunately, we were in the same room and quickly rushed to her side.

"Ebun, what happened? Are you okay?" asked Ife as she put her arms around her shoulders.

"It was a nightmare," Ebun replied, still shaking. "I dreamt that I was alone here, and I couldn't find my way out. It was so scary!"

I had also experienced nightmares before, so I nodded in understanding. "I know how you feel, Ebun. It's really scary to have a bad dream like that."

Ife and I then spent the next few minutes comforting Ebun. We assured her that it was just a dream and that she was safe in her bed. We suggested to her that we could all stay up for a little while and watch a funny movie to help take her mind off the nightmare.

Slowly but surely, Ebun began to calm down and her breathing became steadier.

"Thank you, Ife and Aanu," she said, wiping away her tears. "I don't know what I would do without you guys."

"Don't worry, we'll always be here for you," Ife replied, smiling warmly.

With a little love and assurance, Ebun was finally able to drift back to sleep. She felt safe and secure in the knowledge that she was surrounded by people who loved her. I noticed that she still had the article in her grip. Her hands were sweaty. I waited by her bed to be sure that she was sleeping soundly. When I was certain that everyone was asleep, I got up and sat on her study table and thought about her dream.

She told me that she could not comprehend her dream, but she figured it was about a disease that created panic. I switched on the table lamp, placed the article under it and started reading it.

"Organ transplantation has become the best medical treatment for individuals with end-stage organ failure all around the world. After discussing a variety of legal, ethical, social, and religious perspectives on organ and tissue transplants around the world, including Nigeria in particular, and highlighting abuses and controversies, we concluded that there is no law/legislation supporting organ/tissue transplantation in Nigeria. The government should take steps to protect the poor and vulnerable groups from transplantation tourism and the sale of tissues and organs, as well as address the larger issue of international trafficking in human tissues and organs. An ethics commission should be established to ensure the ethics of cell, tissue, and organ transplantation. A national transplant registry should be developed to oversee and control the country's transplant program."

"There is no regulatory body or laws for organ transplantation?" Ebun had carefully circled that portion. This meant that, more than anything, there should be a law to make people act accordingly. Only then could there be a check and balance on this situation; otherwise, traffickers would be free to run rampant on innocent people. The general public is not in safe hands if there is no law regarding organ transplantation. Hence, corruption thrives in the healthcare department.

I was impressed at the research she had done, but I was worried about her mental health, too. Ebun could not do anything as she was just a little kid. As she was unable to solve the problem and didn't feel good about it, she started making notes in her journal. She noted in her little pink journal whatever she found important or interesting: statistics, statements, acts, bills, and solutions. She told me she could not shake the image of Mum lying on her bed, bleeding off her mind. I paused to consider her dream again for a moment and then started to scan her little pink journal.

"Organ/tissue transplantation has been established as the best therapy option for individuals with end-stage organ failures worldwide. Renal transplantation, for example, is the greatest option for individuals with end-stage renal illness because it provides a higher quality and quantity of life at a lower cost than hemodialysis. Transplanting organs and tissues necessitates significant expenditure in terms of hospital setup and equipment, employees' training, and recurrent financial assistance. The recipient of an organ transplant would need immunosuppressive medication as well as the control of post-transplant infections and cancers, all of which would necessitate funding. Government/community cooperation is required to fund and sustain such a program."

Under that note, Ebun wrote a question with a bright red marker: "It has been 40 years since the first transplant, and they still have not decided to work together? Why is anyone not paying attention?"

Ebun was curious to know why the government and the people had not decided to work together and make this happen. She was not wrong. This was a much-needed collaboration. People need to be aware of the threats they face and how many precious lives are lost due to the lack of safety measures regarding transplantation law.

The government was not taking needed actions in the healthcare sector, and the general public was scared. The healthcare sector is so underfunded that Nigerians lose hope once they contract a severe disease; they believe they are doomed and there is no remedy. What was sickening was that the poor were the source of organs for the rich, but the poor could not get help. They were just there to die or get their organs harvested. I read a cutout from a newspaper in which there was a piece of news about a doctor removing the kidneys of a patient who came to his clinic to treat typhoid.

It was too much for me, so I closed her journal and went back to sleep. I wondered if I would be able to sleep with this information swirling around in my head. No wonder poor Ebun was getting nightmares.

"No wonder people are scared. With no laws to act as checks and balances, who knows what happens when you are given anaesthesia? There was no one they could trust." I woke up to see that Ife was still asleep, but Ebun was already at her desk and talking to herself. She had a glass of orange juice sitting right next to her laptop.

Indeed, People are worried about going to hospitals because they all know about the sickly, illegal organ trade going on. They are scared that their organs could be harvested by corrupt doctors or medical officers. A rich fellow in need of an organ could pay corrupt medical personnel to get what he wants. This could inevitably result in the death of the unsuspecting donor. It truly was a nightmare, and as Ebun kept reading, she felt claustrophobic.

She got up and opened the window for some fresh air. She could see the faint lights of Abuja city from her window. She thought about the people who lived there; people who were silently and helplessly suffering and waiting for the end to come; scared people and people who were being scammed by wolves in lamb's hides.

Our room was lit with glow-in-the-dark stars in the ceiling, and her desk glowed with neon tape.

Reading pages upon pages of news and statistics, Ebun got tired. Her brain was tired, not her eyes. She felt sick after reading what had been going on in her country. She began to picture scenarios that made her feel uncomfortable. She could imagine some poor kid kicking and crying as her mother and some organ traffickers connived to harvest her organs. She imagined one of her sisters being subjected to such a vile act. She felt guilty about being born into a well-off family while her fellow Nigerians suffered in silence.

"Every year, hundreds upon thousands of young Nigerians are trafficked to Europe. They are promised lucrative jobs, only to realise later, much to their dismay, that they were trafficked to illegally harvest their organs. Poor children are made to believe that rich professions awaited them in Europe, but they end up losing their organs to criminal rings."[6],[7]

I saw Ebun holding her hand to her mouth. She could not believe humans could be so evil. Imagining her sisters going to pursue education abroad only to end up getting their organs harvested was the stuff of nightmares.

She felt scared. She got up, closed her window, and sat on her desk again. Her mind and heart were racing. Her heart was beating so loudly that she could hear it. She did not feel safe. Ebun was just a child, and her curiosity led her to this chilling information that was not meant for kids her age. All her research on the health conditions in her country had a great impact on her brain.

She wanted to get on the roof of her house and scream her lungs out. She wanted to tell everyone what was happening in their beloved country and warn human traffickers that she was going to wipe them off the face of the planet. She wanted to scream till she could not speak anymore. The atrocity was too much for her mind to grasp. She wanted to cry and get God's attention.

CHAPTER 4 DISCUSSION QUESTIONS:

1. In Ebun's dream, she witnessed a chaotic and unsettling scene in her neighbourhood. How does the dream reflect her fears and concerns about the healthcare situation in Nigeria?

2. How does Ebun's nightmare affect her, and what does it reveal about her emotional state and the weight of her research on healthcare issues?

3. Ebun's research highlights the lack of regulations and legal framework for organ transplantation in Nigeria. How does this lack of legal oversight contribute to the problems she's researching?

4. How does Ebun's journaling and note-taking help her process the information she discovers, and what questions does she raise about the healthcare system?

5. The information Ebun uncovers about organ trafficking and illegal organ harvesting has a deep impact on her. How does it affect her perception of the world, and what emotions does it evoke in her?

6. What internal conflicts and concerns are Ebun experiencing due to her research, and how does she grapple with the harsh realities she's uncovering about her country's healthcare system?

CHAPTER 5

AANU

D id you hear about it, Ebun? Or did you already know?" Ann asked Ebun, who was busy devouring her sandwich.

"Know what?" Ebun asked.

"The competition! You should have been the first to know since it's about your interest," Ann said, rolling her eyes at her.

"Really? Tell me about it! I love to compete. My dad always tells us that the best way to learn is to compete," Ebun said, giving Ann all her attention.

"There is a writing competition, and it has commenced nationwide. Participants will have to write an essay. Ten winners will emerge from all over Nigeria and whoever wins will be awarded and rewarded," Ann said to build Ebun's interest, but Ebun was still waiting for the catch.

"That is lovely, but tell me, why do you think I'd be interested in it?" Ebun asked her.

"I am glad that you asked," Ann said excitedly. "Ms Olokun-Esin, participants will get a grand prize! You have a competitive spirit, and you are a great writer. I thought you would be interested."

Even though she was not taking part in the competition, Ann was equally excited because she knew that Ebun would be thrilled to hear this news.

Ebun's eyes grew wide as she listened to the details of the competition.

"I will do it! Thanks, Ann. I will take it from here," Ebun said, as she picked up her bag.

"Where are you going?" Ann asked her "To write the best paper in the world!" Ebun said as she departed for the library.

Later that day, in her last class, the teacher announced the competition.

"So, we will be receiving submissions from anyone who wants to compete," the teacher said. "You will be writing on 'The Power of Shared Things.'"

Ebun's mind started racing the minute her teacher gave them the guidelines. After thinking for a minute, she realised that she had the perfect topic, and she had been studying and reading about it for quite some time. Donating organs and tissues for transplantation was the ultimate act of sharing, and there could not be a better topic to write about.

At first, when Ann gave her the news, Ebun was excited, but when she realised that she had the perfect topic, she was beyond excited.

She thought to herself that this could be her chance to share with the world information about the deteriorating state of healthcare in Nigeria. She saw this as a sign from God and got to work.

By the time she got this news, she was already on forums and websites where everyone from around the world was sharing views and news about organ transplantation. This gave her great insight into the topic and her interest grew even stronger. She befriended people her age from different countries and asked them questions so she could write better.

She had a week to write the paper and all she did after school was research and write. We saw her dedication, and Ife and I took care of all her needs while she was busy with her competition. We helped her with homework and did her chores. In the past, Ife never left a chance to tease and annoy her. However, she knew how much the competition meant to her, so she supported her fully and even helped her troubleshoot on Google.

After working hard for days and writing for hours, Ebun finally felt satisfied with her paper. She asked me to proofread it for her. I was pleasantly surprised at her composition and told her that she was going to ace it. She submitted the paper and waited for the outcome. Every day, she'd check the school's soft board for the announcement of the result. She knew that she worked hard, but she still got nervous. She wanted her essay to be the most informed and knowledgeable, and she expected to win the competition and cause a change in her little way by creating awareness.

One day, while she was going for her recess, she saw a big yellow note on the soft board. She stopped to read it, and as she read it, tears rolled down her cheeks and a smile spread on her face. Ebun was one of the ten people from across the country who won the competition. Ann and Lisa saw her standing by the softboard. They stopped to read what she was staring at, and as they read, they started jumping with joy.

"Oh my God! Do you know what this means, Ebun?" Ann could barely contain her excitement. "You are going to China! An all-expense paid trip sponsored by the Chinese Cultural Program for Children."

"For real?" Ebun asked in disbelief.

"Yes, girl! Did you even read the whole info about the competition?" Ann said, laughing.

Ebun was so excited about writing the paper on her current favourite topic that she forgot to read all the information. She was recommended by the school committee to visit China.

When Ebun got home, she told everyone about the outcome of the competition. She threw her bag on the floor once she stepped in through the main door and started calling everyone loudly. When we all gathered around her, she showed us the yellow paper that was stuck on the school's soft board. We were delighted, and our parents were so proud that Ebun began to cry. General Akin Olokun-Esin took her in his arms, squeezed her tight, and congratulated her.

***

"What is a pandemic?" a scared Ebun asked her teacher.

"A pandemic is a widespread occurrence of an infectious disease across an entire country or the world at a particular time," her teacher answered.

"Is it all over the world right now? At home, too?" Ebun asked, holding her teacher's hand, her heart racing at breakneck speed.

"I hope not, love. I hope not," her teacher said, hugging her tightly to her chest.

"I am worried for my family, miss," she told her teacher.

"We all are, honey. We will see them soon," she told Ebun. Ebun slept in her teacher's arms.

When she woke up, she heard that China had declared an emergency due to the mysterious Coronavirus in Wuhan that was spreading drastically. She also learnt that the WHO announced the mysterious Coronavirus-related pneumonia in Wuhan and the Nigerian government was calling its citizens back from China.

Ebun came online immediately after she had breakfast. We had been waiting for her call because Mum was worried. We sat in our living room, our hearts racing as we video-called her. We missed her energy so much and were especially worried about everything that was happening in China.

"Hi, Aanu!" My little sister Ebun's face popped up on the screen.

"Ebun! Hi!" We exclaimed, feeling a small sense of relief flood through us.

"How are you?" Ife chimed in.

"I'm okay. I miss you guys so much," Ebun said, her voice laced with sadness.

"What's wrong? Why do you sound so sad?" Mum said with concern.

"It's just… This virus, Mum. It's everywhere, and I'm so scared," Ebun confessed, feeling tears prick at the corners of her eyes.

"It's okay, my dear. You are safe, and we are all taking precautions back home. You have nothing to worry about," General Akin Olokun-Esin reassured her, a small smile playing on his lips.

"I know, but it's hard not to worry. I wish I could be there with you guys," Ebun said, feeling a lump form in her throat.

"We wish you could be here too, but we know you're doing something important in China. Just make sure you keep safe, okay?" Mum said, her voice firm but filled with love.

"I will, Mama. I love you guys so much," Ebun said, her heart feeling a little lighter.

"We love you too, Ebun. Take care of yourself," Mum said before ending the call.

We sat back, feeling a little better after talking to her. We knew she had to stay strong and make the most of her time in China. We also knew that we would always be there for her no matter what. But if anything, it was an ironic twist of fate that Ebun's worst healthcare fears had caught up with her in faraway China, away from her loved ones. It seemed that the pandemic knew no poor or wealthy kids or even adults. The entire world was on tenterhooks.

Ebun feared that the dream she had might come true and wanted to see her sisters badly. She was also worried about the whole situation. However, after talking to us, she was relieved that we were safe and that we would soon reunite.

After some medical inspection and going through a dozen checkpoints, Ebun and her teachers were cleared to board their flight. The minute they took off, Ebun told us that she fell asleep, hoping to open her eyes in Abuja.

When she woke up, they had already landed. Ebun was excited to see us and her friends and could not wait to tell them about her trip. When she got off the plane, she saw that everyone at the airport was wearing masks. Coronavirus had spread throughout the world in a matter of weeks, and the whole world was going through a tough time. As they drove into town, she saw that the streets were empty, and there were checkpoints everywhere.

It was January 20, 2020. We were told that Ebun would not go home. Instead, she and her teachers would be going to the University of Abuja Teaching Hospital to be quarantined.

"Why are we not going home?" Ebun asked her teacher. "It is for our safety, honey," Ebun's teacher replied. "The government of Nigeria does not want this disease to spread here, too. So, these are safety measures they are taking. Once we are tested and cleared of the virus, we will be allowed to go home."

Ebun's teacher, Stella, was a mother herself, and she was worried for her family, too. Ebun told me that she took special care of her on the trip like her own child. She knew that her children must be missing her badly, and she felt the same for Ebun.

"I want to see my family. I am scared," Ebun told her teacher tearfully.

"Oh, no, honey. Do not cry. Here they come," her teacher said while smiling.

Ebun turned around, and there we were. We came to see her as soon as we knew she was back. She wanted to hug her mother and father tightly, but she could not. There was a glass wall between us. It was a safety precaution, and the staff at the hospital were strict about non-physical contact.

"Why is there trouble wherever you go?" I asked Ebun teasingly. We were all wearing masks, but she knew that we were smiling.

She told us about her trip and when the pandemic broke out. She tried to summarise everything in a minute as she was overcome by the excitement the restriction tried to impose on her. We listened to her, and we were glad that she had the time of her life there.

"I am so jealous of you! Next year, I will write a paper, and I will be the one going to Disneyland," Ife said, pretending to make a sad face.

"Do not be jealous, Ms Olokun-Esin. I will help you write it so you can win just like you helped me," Ebun said, putting her hand on the glass that was between her and Ife. "Have faith!" she added with a smile on her face.

We chatted for an hour, and Ebun shared all the details of her trip with us and how Chinese is such a difficult but interesting language.

"Listen, I want to ask you guys a favour," Ebun said as we prepared to leave her."What is it, honey? Tell me," Mum said with tears in her eyes.

"If I ever die because of the Coronavirus, I want my organs and tissues to be donated across the world. I am volunteering, so please respect my last wish," Ebun said in a confident and mature tone.

Strong words coming from a child this young made everyone at the hospital teary-eyed.

"Promise me, Ife and Aanu. It is my wish. Consider this your sister's will," she said with the most vibrant smile.

She made us cross our hearts. Even though we knew that it was never going to happen, we promised to make sure her wishes were fulfilled. We also promised to come to see her soon again.

CHAPTER 5 DISCUSSION QUESTIONS:

1. How does Ebun's excitement about the writing competition change from the beginning to the end of the chapter? What drives this change?

2. What is the significance of the competition's theme, "The Power of Shared Things," in the context of the story?

3. How does Stacy's paper on wealth inequality contrast with Ebun's essay on organ transplantation? In what ways are they both addressing issues of sharing and inequality?

4. Describe Ebun's experience in China, from her visit to the Great Wall to her time at the Ocean Aquarium. What emotions does she go through during this part of her journey?

5. How does the sudden outbreak of the coronavirus affect Ebun's experience in China and her return home? How does she cope with the fear and uncertainty?

6. What does Ebun's request regarding organ donation reveal about her character, values, and the themes of the story?

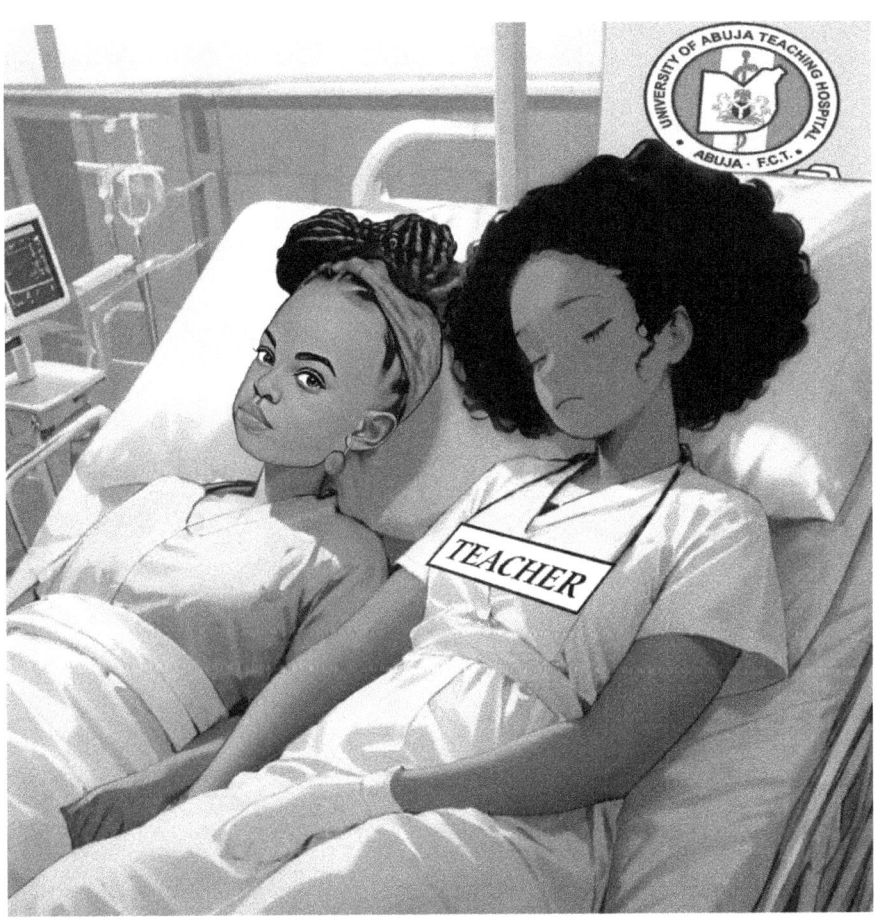

CHAPTER 6

IFE

*I*fe. My name means 'love,' and regardless of what my sisters think, I love Aanu and Ebun a lot.

When we were younger, people told me that I was more active and vibrant, whereas my sister Aanu tended to be more relaxed and composed. I enjoyed intense activities such as sports or dance, while Aanu preferred more conservative hobbies such as reading and painting.

I was 'the crazy one' while Aanu was more reserved. I enjoyed practical jokes and teased my sisters a lot but Aanu was not as comfortable with these types of interactions. However, due to her strong-willed nature, she was resilient and well-equipped e to handle unexpected situations and challenges.

I was competitive, but Aanu had a composed demeanour. That aspect of her made her approach challenges in a more measured and strategic way. While I enjoyed the thrill of competition and the rush of adrenaline that came with winning, Aanu focused on long-term goals and worked steadily toward achieving them.

Despite our different personalities while growing up, Aanu and I learned a lot from each other's strengths. My energetic and mischievous nature brought excitement and fun to my sister's more reserved demeanour, while her strong-willed and composed nature helped ground me and provide stability. This balance was much needed when our family was going through a hard time. I learned later on in life that we made one hell of a team.

As I entered the living room, I saw my sister Aanu sitting on the couch, her eyes fixed on an untouched glass of orange juice. She looked up at me as I approached, and I could see worry written across her face.

"What's wrong?" I asked, taking a seat next to her.

"It's Ebun," she replied, her voice barely above a whisper. "I am worried about what she said and the dream she had."

My heart sank when I also recalled what she said.

"They said she might have contracted COVID-19 and that is why they had to isolate her and her teachers in that special room!"

I could see the tears welling up in Aanu's eyes as she spoke. I put a comforting arm around her and pulled her closer.

"It's going to be okay," I said reassuringly. "Nothing is confirmed, and she is used to saying stuff like that. She's got a wild imagination. Ebun is strong, and she's going to get through this."

Aanu nodded, but I could tell that she was still worried because I was, too. I reached for her glass of orange juice and handed it to her.

"Here, drink this," I said. "It'll make you feel better."

Aanu took the glass and sipped from it, but I could tell that she was still concerned about our little sister.

"I wish there was something we could do for her," she said, her voice breaking.

"We can pray for her," I suggested. "And we can also make her a get-well-soon card to let her know that we're thinking of her."

Aanu's eyes lit up at the suggestion. "That's a great idea!" she exclaimed.

We spent the next hour making the card. Aanu carefully selected the colours and decorations while I helped with the writing. As we worked, I could see Aanu's worries slowly fading away, replaced by a sense of purpose and hope. This was the first time we were working as a team on something; I did not know that this would pave the way for a greater cause.

When we finished, we put the card in an envelope and sealed it.

"Let's go drop this off at the hospital," I said, standing up.

Aanu nodded, and we went to the hospital with our parents, Aanu holding the card tightly. As we walked, I saw the determination in her eyes, and I knew that we would get through the current predicament together as a family.

On our way to the hospital, we found out through our father that Ebun and her teachers were cleared to go home. We went to pick her up from the hospital and Mum hugged her as soon as she was out. We took her home, where we sat talking for hours. Ebun had brought gifts and souvenirs for us and Aanu and I loved them. Ebun was relieved to be home. She missed her bed and the stars that glowed on the sealing.

She fell asleep once her head hit the pillow. She had a sound sleep after days of staying at the strange quarantine centre and woke up to the sound of the alarm. She was excited to go to school and talk to her friends about the trip and get updates on the pandemic.

"Lagos and Kano are the most volatile parts of Nigeria that were hit with Coronavirus, and Abuja is relatively safe," Lisa told Ebun and hugged her. "You were at the epicentre of the pandemic. Thank God you are safe."

"It got really scary at the end of my trip, but I had a blast," Ebun told Lisa, who was listening with full concentration. "When we grow up, we are going to Shanghai. I will have you guys meet the friends I made there, and we will go to the 3D Magic Funhouse, too! It was amazing."

"Wow, did you find it just like we discussed?" Lisa asked.

"It was even cooler than that!" Ebun was beside herself with excitement, reliving her magical trip to China. "My preconceived notions about

China changed after seeing Beijing and Shanghai. It also gave me a new perspective on the rest of the world. I am more eager to travel to places I have never been to. I thought I knew fairly much about China, the country with the world's fastest-growing economy before I went there. However, I did not anticipate the magnificent and stupefying sights of the Olympic facilities and the Great Wall, the scrumptious food, or the insightful conversations I had with the local students I met. I was humbled to learn about a civilisation that has been around for more than 4,000 years and about the warm and welcoming people who live there. I now have a greater understanding of Chinese culture, traditions, and way of life."

"That sounds amazing! I have heard that they are advanced, but I have only seen things about China in movies and shows," Lisa said.

"Exactly! The fact that they are far more sophisticated than we thought surprised me. Beijing's modern architecture gels perfectly with older structures and well-preserved historical sites. I was shocked to see how modern China is the minute I entered the Bird's Nest, the Water Cube, and, subsequently, Tiananmen Square. With their glass towers, fashionable residents, and bustling streets, Beijing and Shanghai's urban regions resemble Chicago or New York City in certain ways, just like in the movies."

Ebun concluded as she finished the rest of her milkshake. She was making slurping sounds to annoy Ann, who was sitting next to them and scribbling in her notebook.

She looked at Ebun and asked, "What are kids like there?"

"They are just like us!" Ebun said, raising eyebrows. "They are fun-loving and smart. However, one thing that I noted about them is that they place value on morals and principles more than we do. They are much more disciplined. From my contacts with numerous students from the various schools I visited, I discovered that they prioritise honesty and punctuality. My friends in China told me that our future professional development and success are ultimately determined by the image we develop of ourselves over the years. To build their brands, many local businessmen are big on integrity and diligence."

"Is it a good place to live?" Lisa asked her as she closed her notebook.

"Good? It is awesome! China is a terrific place for anyone looking to meet new people, both Chinese nationals and foreigners. The Chinese people are often quite cordial and helpful. Locals will constantly strive to assist you in day-to-day activities, even if your Chinese is bad. Chinese folks tend to be quite reserved when you first meet them, but getting through that is worthwhile."

Ebun was out of breath and started coughing a little as her throat felt dry. She drank water from her bottle and continued. "China offers various opportunities for foreigners. This may be due to the economic boom the country is experiencing or the fact that the government is opening up the country to tourism. Some agencies monitor the job market regularly, and they post job adverts daily. You can easily get a job offer while merely walking down the street. Steady growth and developments occur daily in major Chinese cities, hence creating surplus opportunities."

The recess bell rang and they began to leave for their classes.

"So, it is final. We are going to China together when we graduate high school, okay?" Ann said, jumping up and down as she walked.

Ann and Ebun said "Deal!" in unison and high-fived each other before entering their class.

The Coronavirus was spreading globally. As I was watching the news with Mum, on January 21, the CDC confirmed the first US Coronavirus case. The Seattle region was worst hit by an early U.S. outbreak in the months that followed. In four weeks, 39 residents of Kirkland's Life Care Center passed away from virus-related complications. Some of those who died in January 2020 from COVID-19 were unaware of it at the time. They had their death certificates altered to reflect that the virus was the cause of their death.

Between January 21 and February 23, 2020, public health organisations in the United States reported 14 coronavirus illnesses, and all of the patients diagnosed had visited China. On February 26, the first non-travel case was confirmed in California, and on February 29, the first U.S. death was announced.

People in Nigeria were ignorant as they thought that this disease could not affect them or that it would be contained early enough. However, when they discovered that it had made its way to the US and other developed countries, everyone started to panic.

In Lagos State, Nigeria, the Federal Ministry of Health confirmed a coronavirus case. It was the first case reported in Nigeria since the outbreak started in China in January 2020. The case was confirmed on February 27, 2020.

An Italian national, who works in Nigeria, returned to Lagos for work on February 25, 2020, from Milan, Italy. He tested positive for the virus at the Lagos University Teaching Hospital's Virology Laboratory, a component of the Nigeria Centre for Disease Control's Laboratory Network. The patient was being treated at the Infectious Disease Hospital in Yaba, Lagos, and was clinically stable with no significant symptoms.[9]

At the same time, a Chinese scientist confirmed COVID-19 human-to-human transmission. The chairman of the National Health Commission team and a respiratory expert, Zhong Nanshan, verified that two cases of infection in China's Guangdong province were due to human-to-human transmission and that medical personnel had also contracted the disease.

Concerns grew as cases were confirmed in Beijing, Shanghai, and the southern province of Guangdong. The Chinese government was worried because more than 400 million people were scheduled to travel both domestically and internationally during the Lunar New Year holiday.[10]

Ebun was, however, feeling rejuvenated after her visit. She visited a foreign country for the first time in her life and her experience was memorable in all aspects. She felt tired due to all the travelling and her coughing kept getting worse by the day.

Her school announced that her paper won the best paper of the ten selected papers from Nigeria for the Chinese Cultural Program. This was a proud moment for Ebun and her friends.

Ebun's paper was voted the best since she started her research early and got her information from different students from her school and the people she met on online forums, people from various countries like Spain, Iran, Saudi Arabia, Germany, USA, Ghana, Kenya, South Africa, India, Brazil, and Korea.

Her school awarded Ebun a merit certificate of achievement. Our family, Ebun's teachers, and all her school friends attended a small ceremony in her honour. It was a proud moment for our parents as they saw their youngest daughter shine the brightest in a sea of students.

Ebun gave a wholesome speech in which she praised and thanked her friends who helped her out, her family who supported her and allowed her to gain the valuable experience of visiting China, and her teachers who were with her on her trip and took care of her when the outbreak happened. General Akin Olokun-Esin smiled at her little Ebun, and Mum was proud to see her daughter on stage. She knew that her future was bright; however, she felt that something was wrong. She observed that during her speech, she was coughing mildly. Being a loving mother, she feared the worst. She held her daughters dear and would sacrifice her life for them.

CHAPTER 6 DISCUSSION QUESTIONS

1. How would you describe the relationship between Ife, Aanu, and Ebun? What roles do they play in each other's lives?

2. In what ways do Ife and Aanu complement each other's personalities? How do their differences contribute to their bond as sisters?

3. How does the news of Ebun possibly having contracted COVID-19 affect Aanu and Ife? How did they react to the situation?

4. What role does hope and resilience play in this chapter? How do Ife and Aanu support each other during challenging times?

5. How does Ebun's experience in China change her perspective on the world and different cultures? What aspects of her trip stood out to her the most?

6. The chapter introduces the global spread of the COVID-19 pandemic. How did people in Nigeria initially perceive the virus, and how did that perception change as it spread worldwide?

7. Discuss the significance of Ebun's recognition for her paper on the Chinese Cultural Program. How did her family and school celebrate her achievement?

CHAPTER 7

IFE

We were downstairs with our parents while Ebun was sleeping. She had been feeling tired since she returned from school. She woke up to heavy congestion in her chest. Her star-studded ceiling did not provide her any comfort. She was gasping for air and felt like she was breathing through a needle. Her chest felt heavy, and after trying to catch her breath for a few minutes, she cried out for help.

"I can't breathe, I can't breathe!" Ebun said as she stumbled towards the door, her voice barely audible. As she walked towards the door, her hand touched a glass cup that sat at the edge of her study table. The cup fell to the ground and made an ear-splitting sound in our quiet house. The fragments of glass spread across the marble floor.

The sound of glass breaking was piercing, and Aanu and I ran towards her room immediately. When we came into Ebun's room, we saw her lying on the floor gasping for air.

"Help me! I can't breathe…" Ebun tried to talk.

We were terrified to see her in such distress. We helped her to get downstairs as we shouted for our parents to get up and help.

Our father, General Akin Olokun-Esin, was about to sleep when he heard us shouting, so he ran outside. Somehow, he knew that something had happened to Ebun. He knew what happened once he saw Ebun. He picked her up and ran outside. He told us to stay at home, wear masks, and disinfect ourselves while he drove Ebun straight to the hospital. Later, Father told us that it was one of the longest drives of his life. As he sped on, he kept thinking about his daughter and how she was the smartest and most loving of all three.He took her back to the University of Abuja Teaching Hospital, where she was quarantined and kept under observation. The sad thing about being quarantined was that Ebun could not even be in the same room with her family. Dad stood outside, just hoping and praying to God that his daughter would survive.

"Is she going to be okay?" Dad asked the doctor who emerged from Ebun's room. Even though he was a strong man, his voice was starting to shake.

"I am afraid Ebun has been infected," the doctor said and paused for our father to process the terrifying news.

"Ebun has been infected with Coronavirus. We are trying to keep her stable for now and observing her. We are doing the best we can."

The doctor's response was not satisfactory. Our parents decided to give their daughter the best treatment that was possible in Abuja since Ebun could not travel abroad due to travel restrictions.

Ebun was far from being better. Her health began to deteriorate at an alarming rate, and she was constantly under observation by doctors at the hospital. She was coughing uncontrollably, and her breathing had gotten worse. Everyone was praying for little Ebun's recovery. When her classmates found out about her condition, they were very scared. They missed her, so they wrote her letters.

"Dear Ebun, I hope that you are doing better now. Ann and I are getting bored. We thought a lot about getting a new third friend, but then we decided that we only wanted you. Get well and come back soon so we can enjoy school. It does not feel the same without you. See you soon. Lisa"

Mum had tears in her eyes as she read the letters and cards that Ebun's classmates had sent to her. Aanu and I were sad and worried for our sister. The house did not feel the same without her.

We were all at the hospital, but Dad had just left to get food for us when the doctors told Aanu and me that our sister's vitals were not looking good. Immediately, we called our father who returned within a few minutes. When he met the doctors, they told him that they were doing all they could to save her, but they were helpless since there was no vaccine for Coronavirus.

Our mum was heartbroken. Just a few days ago, she was so proud of her daughter. She was joyful, and now she was praying to God for a miracle. No amount of money could help us. We couldn't do anything to get rid of Ebun's ailment.

Ebun's health kept worsening at an aggressive pace. Everyone at the hospital was in shock. Our happy life had suddenly turned into a nightmare. We were consoling our mother when a doctor approached us. He had a mortifying look on his face.

"I am sorry, Mr and Mrs Olokun-Esin. Ebun could not make it," the doctor said sadly.

Silence fell in the waiting area. Our mum stopped sobbing and stared at the doctor. Our father's eyes were filled with tears, too. We could not believe what had happened. Aanu and I hugged our parents, who were now crying loudly. Everyone in the hospital was teary. They had met Ebun when she first came to the hospital directly from China. She was not sick back then. They all interacted with her, so they knew what a gem of a kid she was.

"Her will…" Mum muttered. "Her last wish… She wanted to help others. My daughter was an angel. She wanted to help people by donating her organs. Don't you remember when we were here the last time?" she said through quivering lips to our father.

We remembered what Mum was referring to as Aanu and I held our mother's hands. When she looked at us, we nodded at her. We all knew how passionate Ebun was about writing her paper and how worried she was about the subject of her paper. We wanted to fulfil her wishes. We talked to the doctor so that they could make arrangements.

We made a donor card. It was not difficult to make because Ebun had begun to champion the cause of donating organs and tissues to needy patients before passing away. She had written a paper that was judged as the best paper on the topic, and it was pretty clear what she would have wanted. She was clear about her wish and we respected it.

The news of Ebun's demise broke out, and the entire Nigerian media besieged the hospital. Our parents were grieving and busy with the legal process with doctors, so we, her sisters, decided to talk to the media. Aanu told them that Ebun believed in love and prosperity. She wanted to donate her organs and tissues to anyone who needed them. We told everyone that this was the time to get together and help each other out.

Even though we were miserable, we talked sensibly and with facts. We answered all the questions about how the organs and tissues would be donated through the International Registry on Organ Donation and Transplantation as well as the International Society for Organ Donation and Procurement.

"As Ebun wanted, we are donating her organs to the needy so lives can be saved. We have made a list after carrying out tests to find the right matches for Ebun's organs, and we would like to tell everyone about the recipients.

"Ebun's kidneys and pancreas will be transported to New York City, US, within 24-36 hours. An orphan whose name is Adam Garfield will be getting them. Her liver will be transported to Dusseldorf, Germany, within 8–12 hours, and her corneas will be sent to Saudi Arabia so that a young girl by the name of Nisa can experience this world to the fullest."

***

The classroom was a sombre atmosphere as the students mourned Ebun's death. The class teacher, wanting to guide her students through the grieving process, decided to address the class about writing condolence notes.

She stood in front of the classroom and took a deep breath. Her expression radiated empathy and understanding.

She began: "Today, we are going to talk about writing condolence notes. I know that the idea of writing such a note can be intimidating and overwhelming, especially during this difficult time. However, I want you to understand how important it is for you to express your support and offer comfort to the family of Ebun."

She paused for a moment so her words could sink in and then continued, "Writing a condolence note can also be how you process your feelings of loss. That way, you can reflect and express your sympathy and love for the departed."

The teacher's gentle tone conveyed a sense of reassurance to the grieving students. She understood that they may not know what to say, but she encouraged them to try.

"I know that finding the right words may feel daunting, but you must remember that the most significant thing is that you make the effort. The family of Ebun will greatly appreciate your sincerity and support during this challenging time."

The teacher proceeded to provide some guidance on how to write a condolence note. She offered suggestions on how to express sympathy, share fond memories, or simply offer a listening ear. She emphasised the importance of personalising the message and acknowledging the unique bond each student had with Ebun.

"As you write your condolence notes," the teacher concluded, "remember that your words hold immense power to comfort and provide solace. Take your time, reflect on your feelings, and offer your condolences with love and sincerity. Remember that we are here for each other, and together, we can navigate through this difficult period."

The students listened attentively and absorbed the teacher's words of wisdom and guidance. They felt a sense of relief knowing that their attempts, no matter how simple, would bring comfort to the grieving family. Inspired by their teacher's compassion, they began to gather their thoughts, ready to pour their hearts into writing their condolence notes for their beloved Ebun.

Hoda was crying her eyes out over Ebun's sad demise. She told her father, who was a Saudi diplomat, about Ebun's death and will. Gulsan, a softly spoken girl often mistaken for shy, was, in truth, deeply introverted. She gently wrapped her arms around Hoda's neck, using her sleeve to dab away the tears. Thoughts of Aitzaz Hasan's story, as recounted by her parents, flooded her mind.

In the rugged mountains of northwest Pakistan, on a cold morning in January, a brave story unfolded. Aitzaz Hasan, only 15 years old, was punished to stand outside of his class for showing up late for school. It was a normal day for him as he and two of his friends stood outside of their class, giggling at the little jokes they made, until he noticed something strange: a man he had never seen before wearing a vest. Aitzaz knew right away who he was, a suicide bomber. The strange man who scared his friends did not do the same for Aitzaz. As his friends decided to run, Aitzaz did not. They urged him to run with them, but he knew the massacre that would unfold if he did. "I'm going to stop him. He is going to school to kill my friends," Aitzaz bravely spoke those words and ran towards the suicide bomber, who had a detonator in his hand. He put up a fight with the suicide bomber, and as the bomber realized his plan failed, he set off the bomb, killing himself and a hero known as Aitzaz Hasan. But because of him, many others were safe that day. News of Aitzaz's bravery spread fast. People everywhere called him a hero. Even though Aitzaz's family was sad, they were proud of what he did. His father's words about Aitzaz's bravery touched everyone in the country.

Gulsan had been just a toddler when the bomb blast shattered her world. Following a grueling two-year journey at IVF (in Vitro fertilization), they eventually turned to an anonymous egg donor from an egg bank to conceive her. The expenses incurred to bring Gulsan into existence, amidst the devastation of a suicide bomb blast and the subsequent loss of her hearing, forced her parents to leave Pakistan for Nigeria. The tragic event that claimed Aitzaz Hasan's life had unfolded at the very school where her parents served as teachers. Thankfully, Gulsan's hearing was eventually restored, thanks to the intervention of specialists at a Nigerian hospital, preventing her from experiencing permanent sensorineural hearing loss. Hoda told her father about Ebun's character and how she was an innocent and intelligent kid. Her father was also an advisor to King Salman of Saudi. When he spoke to the king about Ebun's story, the king of Saudi was impressed by Ebun's courage and extremely grateful that she donated her corneas to a girl in Saudi.

Once he took the decision, the Saudi King, along with many of his cabinet members, decided to address the nation. In his speech, he encouraged the public to follow his example and contribute to saving lives. He told the whole nation that all citizens and residents are eligible to register for the lists of donors using an online link.

The king was so impressed and touched by Ebun's story that he invited us, her sisters, to visit Saudi. Aanu and I knew that Ebun's last wish was to make waves. For us to achieve her vision, we had to take all the opportunities and help that we could get.

After getting permission and blessings from our parents, we left Nigeria immediately with the corneas in the king's private jet. Coincidentally, the recipient of these corneas was the daughter of one of the king's generals in the army. Nisa needed a keratoplasty procedure done to get her corneas replaced with Ebun's new corneas, which were not damaged like Nisa's from an eye infection.

When Aanu and I arrived at the airport, we were received by the general with a reception worthy of a head of state. After the warm reception, we talked to the Crown Prince about our mission to fulfil Ebun's wishes and vision. In fulfilment of her wish, her heart would go to a boy whose name had been on the recipient's list for a long time. Her heart was airlifted to the boy in a hospital in Nasarawa State by a drone made by a Nigerian-American engineer, who was in the US. The remaining body parts, including Ebun's lungs, were shared in

Nigeria.

When we received a call from Iran, we were taken aback. The news of a substantial amount of money being offered for Ebun's organs left us stunned. We couldn't believe what we heard. However, our father's response was resolute: "Her organs are not for sale!"

Indeed, Iran has a legal framework for the sale of organs, and it might be the only country in the world with such a framework. We knew that, in Iran, a government foundation facilitates the registration of both buyers and sellers, matches them up and sets a fixed price of $4,600 per organ. It was astonishing to know that more than 30,000 kidney transplants have been performed in Iran through this process since 1993.

However, for our family, the decision was clear; money could never replace the value we placed on our beloved sister. Ebun's organs were not a commodity to be traded or sold for financial gain. We understood this deeply and stood firm in our conviction.

The room was heavy with grief as our family sat together, finding solace in each other's presence during this devastating period. Our parents' eyes were red and swollen from continuous weeping, their hearts burdened with the weight of their loss. Amid their sorrow, the phone rang and pierced the air with its shrill sound.

Our mother reached for the phone and answered the call, her voice trembling with pain. At the other end of the line was a representative from the Medical Ethics body, whose words would bring both surprise and bewilderment to our shattered lives. The representative began: "Good evening. I am calling on behalf of the Medical Ethics body. We recently learned about your daughter's selfless act of becoming an organ donor, and we would like to express our deepest appreciation for her noble gesture."

Mum listened intently as the representative from the Medical Ethics body spoke. He relayed the words of Dr Chike Okolie, who was the head of the body. The weight of their proposal settled upon her, and she found herself grappling with the moral and societal implications of such an initiative.

"Dr Okolie believes that paying for the funeral expenses of organ donors is ethically justified," the representative continued, his voice steady and filled with conviction. "He emphasises that no harm can come to the donor, and this gesture would be a form of recognition from society and a way to acknowledge the immense value of the selfless acts of organ donors."

Mum considered the words carefully; she recognised the truth in the ethical justification presented. However, she couldn't help but question the potential consequences and the impact it might have on societal perceptions of organ donation. The notion of a pilot scheme to test public response intrigued her, hinting at a possible shift in cultural attitudes and practices.

With a mix of curiosity and concern, she spoke softly, "I understand the reasoning behind Dr Okolie's belief, and I appreciate the innovative approach. But can we truly project all the implications of such a scheme? What would it mean for future perceptions of organ donation and the grieving process?"

The representative listened attentively and acknowledged the weightiness of her words. "We recognise the complexity of the issue," he responded earnestly. "That is why we believe a pilot scheme is necessary—to gauge public response, assess the impact on organ donation rates and, most importantly, ensure that it aligns with the values and beliefs of our society."

Our mother nodded, her mind filled with conflicting thoughts and emotions. She admired the forward-thinking approach and the potential impact it could have on addressing the shortage of organs for transplantation. At the same time, she couldn't ignore the deep-rooted traditions and cultural beliefs that shaped her understanding of grief and mourning.

"Thank you for considering my daughter's noble act and sharing this proposal with us," she finally replied, her voice tinged with a mixture of appreciation and caution. "While I cannot personally accept the offer, I believe it is worth considering. Let us tread carefully and show utmost respect for our cultural values and the experiences of those affected by this scheme."

The representative from the Medical Ethics body expressed gratitude for her thoughtful response. He responded with empathy and understanding and expressed his deep respect for the family's decision. He acknowledged the importance of cultural customs and assured our parents that they would honour and respect their choice.

They understood the weight of tradition and the need to carefully consider it in such matters. The conversation marked the beginning of an ongoing dialogue as society grappled with the intricate balance between cultural practices and the evolving landscape of medical ethics.

Everyone was crying. People pass away and their families cry. However, in Ebun's case, the whole nation cried. They had lost a child whose future was bright and whose mission was to save humanity. Her heart-wrenching story was relayed on every major news channel, and it soon went viral.

There were a lot of people at Ebun's funeral, from doctors, janitors, Ebun's teachers, and friends, and they all wept for her. They were proud of her but sad that she left so early. They had so much respect in their hearts for Ebun.

Most of Ebun's classmates made the sombre journey to attend her funeral, a solemn event that held deep significance in Yoruba culture. Those who didn't come simply adhered to the tradition that parents should not outlive their children. In the Yoruba tradition, it is an abomination for parents to know the burial site of their offspring.

The Yoruba people believe that children who witness funeral services may have their ability to mourn affected. Some say that disallowing children from witnessing funerals can lead to regret in later years. Despite this cultural norm, there is a growing consensus among experts that children should be allowed to attend funerals or memorial services if they feel emotionally capable of doing so.

Attending a funeral helps children to process the reality of death, grieve, and say their final goodbyes. However, we must consider a child's emotions and fears. If a child is scared or uncomfortable with the idea of attending a funeral, they should not force them. Instead, parents and guardians can encourage them to honour the departed in a way that feels meaningful and comfortable to the child. The child ought to experience the benefits that come with grieving alongside loved ones and be able to recall meaningful memories shared with the deceased. Therefore, those classmates who felt prepared and emotionally capable of attending Ebun's funeral service gathered together to honour her memory and bid her a final farewell. The ceremony afforded them the avenue to express their grief, share in the collective mourning process, and find solace in the presence of loved ones.

Julia, a little Dutch girl in Ebun's class, was so heartbroken at her death. She was Ebun's friend, and she had witnessed many funeral services in her country. She was inspired by a Dutch artist and poet, Frank Starik, who created a collection of poems called "Lonely Funeral Poems."

In these solemn ceremonies, typically held with a group of pallbearers, a designated civil servant, and the poets, the Lonely Funeral Poems served as a way to honour and remember the departed individuals.

Moved by the tragedy of Ebun's untimely death, Julia volunteered to read the funeral eulogy and took on the role of funeral director. Julia, with the support of Frank Stark's poems, helped ensure that Ebun's funeral was heartfelt and filled with meaningful tributes.

Alara had been numb since she heard about Ebun's untimely death. She stood at the entrance of the funeral parlour, her heart heavy with grief. The news of Ebun's sudden demise had shattered her world and left her with a deep sense of loss. As tears welled up in her eyes, Alara clutched her sketchbook tightly against her chest and sought solace in her art.

Ebun had always been Alara's muse, her inspiration. They had spent countless hours together, sharing dreams, laughter, and a love for creativity.

Alara knew she had only one way to express the depth of her emotions and pay tribute to her dear friend: the creation of a funeral portrait.

With trembling hands, Alara found a quiet corner in the parlour. Surrounded by the hushed whispers and sombre atmosphere, she opened her sketchbook and stared at the blank page before her. Memories of Ebun flooded her mind—their adventures shared artistic endeavours and the radiant smile that could brighten the darkest of days.

Taking a deep breath, Alara let her pencil glide across the page. She poured her heart and soul into each stroke, infusing the lines with her love for Ebun and the profound sorrow she felt at her loss. The image slowly took shape, capturing the essence of her friend—the gentle curve of her face, the sparkle in her eyes, and the warmth of her spirit.

Time seemed to stand still as Alara immersed herself in the portrait. She was lost in a world where only she and Ebun existed—a world where their bond was eternal and unbreakable. Hours passed but Alara remained focused, determined to bring her friend back to life, if only on paper.

Finally, as she completed the final stroke, Alara stepped back, her heart both heavy and light. The funeral portrait of Ebun lay before her—a masterpiece born out of love, grief and a deep longing for her friend's presence. It captured the essence of who Ebun was: a prodigious artist, a bright soul, and a cherished friend.

As the funeral service commenced, Alara gently carried the portrait to the front of the room, careful not to smudge the delicate lines. She placed it on an easel, allowing it to stand proudly, a testament to the beauty and talent that was extinguished far too soon.

Throughout the service, mourners were drawn to Alara's creation. The portrait became a focal point—a visual representation of the joy and vitality that Ebun had brought into their lives. It evoked both tears and smiles as people were reminded of the indelible mark Ebun left on their hearts.

As our parents saw their daughter for the last time for her funeral procession, they also saw that everyone stood and looked at Ebun. They all saluted her for being a bigger person. She was bigger than everyone, even in death. She lived up to her name and inspired people to love one another. Although Ebun was gone, she remained alive in the hearts of so many people. She had become a legend overnight, and, as she desired, she had become one of the most powerful women in Nigeria.

The classroom still wore a sombre atmosphere as Ebun's classmates gathered together after her funeral. The absence of her vibrant energy was palpable, and a heavy silence hung in the air. But amidst the grief, there was a shared desire to remember Ebun in the most joyful way possible.

Stacy, with tears still brimming in her eyes, cleared her throat and spoke up, "Guys, remember that time when Ebun told our teacher that her dog ate her homework although she didn't have a dog?" A little smile formed at the corners of her lips as she recalled the memory.

A few stifled chuckles escaped the lips of her classmates, breaking the silence that had engulfed the room. Slowly, the tension started to ease, and the healing power of humour began to weave its magic.

Amidst the laughter, memories of Ebun's mischievousness and infectious laughter flooded their minds. One by one, they started sharing their individual funny moments they had with her. Tales of pranks played, hilarious classroom antics and unforgettable adventures spilt forth, each anecdote fuelling more laughter and bringing their beloved friend back to life in their hearts.

As the room filled with laughter and tears mixed with smiles, the weight of grief seemed to momentarily lift. In those moments, they were reminded that despite the pain of loss, life was still filled with moments of joy and levity. The shared humour created a sense of camaraderie among Ebun's classmates and fostered a bond that unified them in their collective memories and experiences. They found solace in the knowledge that they could find moments of respite through laughter, even in the face of loss.

It was in those moments that they realised the profound truth that humour and laughter are powerful tools to help manage grief. By finding humour and embracing laughter, they could navigate the complexities of their emotions and find a sense of comfort.

In that classroom, Ebun's spirit seemed to linger as if she were laughing along with them, encouraging them to find joy even in the darkest of times. Through their shared laughter, they kept her memory alive, and in turn, she continued to bring smiles to their faces.

As the laughter subsided and the room fell into a more peaceful silence, Ebun's classmates felt a renewed sense of strength and resilience. They understood that humour could be a beacon of light, guiding them through the process of grief and helping them find solace in the memories they held dear.

And so, they sat together, hearts still heavy but spirits lifted, cherishing the gift of laughter that Ebun had left behind. In those moments of shared joy, they found comfort, healing, and the realisation that humour, even in the face of loss, had the power to heal and bring them closer.

CHAPTER 7 DISCUSSION QUESTIONS

1. What major health issue did Ebun face in this chapter, and how did it affect her?

2. Describe the family's reaction when Ebun's health deteriorates. How did General Olokun-Esin, her father, respond to the situation?

3. How does Ebun's last wish, as mentioned in this chapter, impact her family's decisions regarding organ donation?

4. Explain the significance of the Medical Ethics body's proposal to pay for the funeral expenses of organ donors. How does Ebun's family react to this proposal?

5. What cultural and societal customs or practices related to funerals are discussed in the chapter? How do they affect the characters' actions and decisions?

6. How does humour play a role in helping Ebun's classmates cope with their grief? Why is this important in the grieving process?

7. Discuss the impact of Ebun's actions and her vision on her family, her classmates, and even the nation as a whole.

8. Reflect on the story of Aitzaz Hasan mentioned by Gulsan. How does his act of bravery compare to Ebun's actions, and what lessons can be drawn from both their stories?

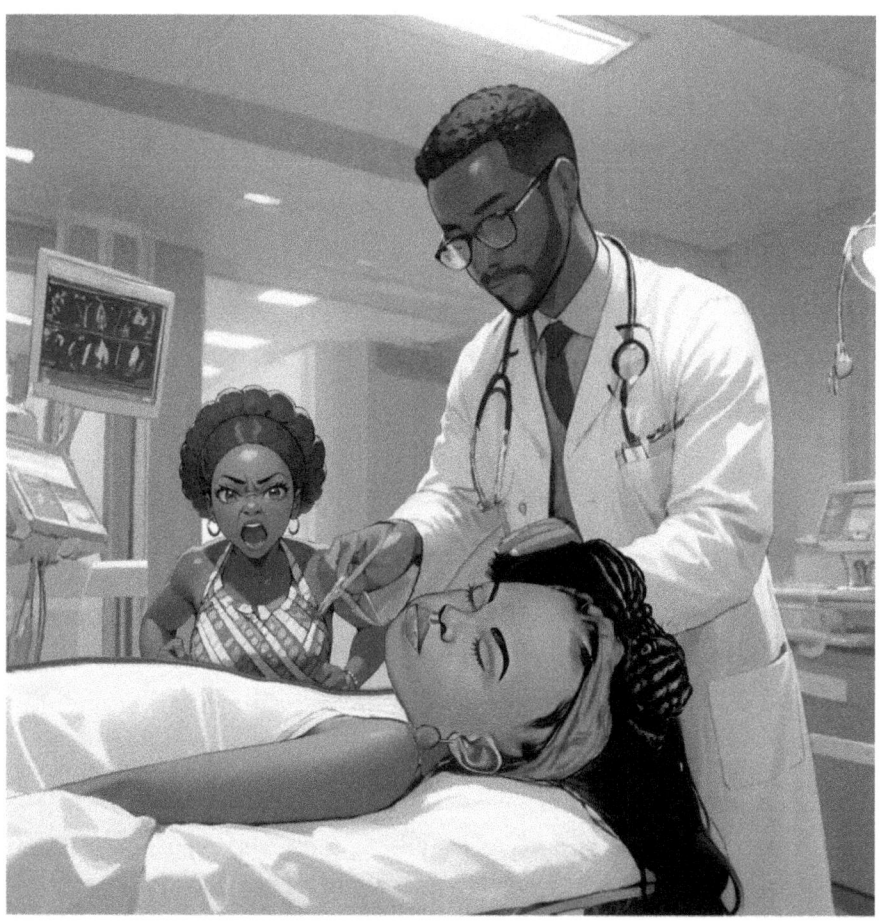

CHAPTER 8

IFE

A hospital radiologist in Abuja studied images sent from China that showed lung damage in Covid-19 patients. The Nigerian doctor had never seen a pattern like it in tuberculosis or any other respiratory illness. Around the patient's lungs, there were white, rounded patches. He and a co-worker called them "peripheral ground glass". Although they could see the tsunami coming, they didn't know how powerful it would be.

Soon, hospitals were inundated with patients suffering from conditions that had previously only been footnotes in reports from China and Europe. Hospitals anticipated the COVID-19 "cytokine storm" of inflammatory responses and respiratory problems. They did not, however, anticipate seeing as many patients with multi-system organ failure, including the hardening of the heart's walls, severe renal failure, and brain blood clots.

The Nigerian government declared an emergency and put in place heavy restrictions. The whole world was in the dark clutches of this new disease. People were strictly advised to wear face masks around other people since the disease was airborne and was spreading at an exponential rate. Soon, lockdowns were in place, too. There was a complete travel ban. All forms of public transport were halted and people were advised not to leave home except to visit the hospital in case of an emergency or get essentials for their households.

Anyone found outside without a mask was punished and fined. A wave of terror spread over the whole world, including Nigeria. The coronavirus had brought the human race to its knees. Scientists and doctors worldwide struggled to find a cure to slow down the climbing death rates or stop it entirely.

Social distancing soon became a norm, as people were not allowed to sit in groups of as few as three. Restaurants and all public places were closed, along with schools, colleges, and universities for an unprecedented time.

Nigeria experienced a significant surge in crime rates during the Covid-19 pandemic. The economic repercussions of the crisis left many people unemployed and struggling to survive. Faced with the fear that they might not only fall victim to the virus but also to starvation, desperation led some individuals to engage in criminal activities.

Among those affected was an 11-year-old boy named Pilal. He was part of a group of children who resorted to begging for alms and food on the streets during the pandemic. Pilal's circumstances were influenced by a prevalent Islamic educational practice in the northern part of Nigeria known as *almajiri*. In this system, parents often sent their young children, mostly boys, aged four to twelve, to distant places to receive Quranic education.

The *almajiri* system had its implications, including the absence of parental care and its reliance on begging for alms for the survival of its pupils. As the situation worsened, Pilal and his group joined looters who targeted state warehouses in the Federal Capital Territory, where COVID-19 relief supplies were stockpiled. Authorities denied allegations of hoarding or planning to sell the supplies.

Unfortunately, during one of their ventures, Pilal carelessly crossed the road without checking for oncoming traffic and was hit by our father's car. Dad, realising the severity of the situation, immediately parked his car and rushed Pilal to the nearest hospital. However, the hospital didn't have sufficient beds, and despite the medical staff's efforts, Pilal passed away five days later.

The cause of Pilal's death was attributed to haemophilia, a rare genetic bleeding disorder that affects the blood's clotting process due to deficiencies in certain clotting factors. This condition predominantly affects males. Filled with a sense of responsibility and empathy, Dad managed to track down Pilal's parents through his Quranic teacher and offered them financial compensation.

Our father gave Pilal's parents a sum of N150,000, while the Quranic teacher received N50,000. Overwhelmed by this unexpected act of kindness and the substantial amount of money, one they had never handled, Pilal's parents expressed their profound gratitude. They were so touched by the gesture that they pleaded with the Quranic teacher to accept another one of their children into the *almajiri* system. It is worth noting that Pilal's father had two wives, both of whom were physically challenged (lame). Each morning, he would transport them to strategic locations on his motorbike for alms begging, as that was their only source of livelihood.

The plight of *almajiri* boys like Pilal is often exacerbated by the lack of proper care and parenting. Many of these children grow up in challenging environments and risk being influenced by various Islamic extremist and violent groups. The cycle continues, perpetuating the need for comprehensive reforms to address the root causes of their vulnerability and provide them with opportunities for a better future.

During the pandemic, there were riots and panic in countries throughout the world. Coronavirus was not only taking a toll on human lives, but it was also damaging the world economy and impoverishing people. Great harm was done to economic growth by the measures put in place to stop the spread of the virus and provide relief for the frail and overburdened health systems.

COVID-19 caused an unprecedented worldwide crisis. In addition to taking a heavy human toll, the global health crisis was also contributing to the worst economic downturn since the Second World War. In that year, there were predictions that both the global economy and per capita incomes would contract, plunging millions into abject poverty.

The economic fallout hampered the ability of nations to adequately address the health and economic implications of the epidemic. Nearly half of all low-income nations were already in debt crisis or were in high danger of plunging into it even before the spread of COVID-19, leaving them with little fiscal room to aid the poor and vulnerable who were struck hardest.

Amid all the chaos Aanu and I were travelling the world and giving interviews as Ebun's story of bravery and empathy reached millions. Aanu and I were invited to many talk shows and news channels so we could tell Ebun's story and inspire people around the world. We told people how a girl as young as ten years old changed the lives of six kids around the world with her single act of kindness and how this act made a huge impact worldwide.

As we journeyed, we witnessed the profound impact of Ebun's story, reaching millions and resonating deeply within communities far and wide. In Saudi Arabia, the echoes of her selflessness reverberated particularly loudly. Here, the involvement of Saudi Arabia's King Salman and Crown Prince Mohammed bin Salman in the organ donor program stood as a critical component of the Saudi Center for Organ Transplantation, an institution tirelessly championed by King Salman. Their dedication aimed to alleviate the suffering of countless patients grappling with kidney failure and other organ-related ailments.

Ebun's case not only garnered significant attention and support but also catalyzed existing efforts within Saudi Arabia. King Salman and Crown Prince Mohammed bin Salman, who had long been advocates for organ donations and transplants, found their campaign propelled to new heights by Ebun's inspiring story.

In 1982, a fatwa (religious edit) by the Senior Ulama Commission concerning organ donation and transplantation granted permission to remove an organ or part thereof from a dead person and allow for the donation of the organ, or part of it, to a living person. King Salman established SCOT, Saudi Arabia's primary organization for transplants, in 1984. This laid the foundation for the country's commitment to organ donation and transplantation. Fast forward to March 2021, when Saudi Arabia's cabinet approved the human organ donation regulation. This regulation, sanctioned by the Shoura Council in September 2019, allows for the transfer, cultivation, preservation, and development of organs to preserve human life. It also protects the rights of those involved in organ donation and transplantation, licenses health facilities, and defines their responsibilities to prevent exploitation or trafficking in human organs. Ebun's donation significantly contributed to attracting more people to join King Salman and Crown Prince Mohammed bin Salman in their vision for organ donations and transplants.

Saudi Crown Prince Mohammed bin Salman introduced us to what is deemed the world's largest floating structure ever built, named Pangeos. The $8 billion master project, a turtle-shaped terayacht, measured 2,000 feet at its widest point. It will comprise various hotels, shopping centers, parks, ship and aircraft ports, and other facilities needed to house up to 60,000 inhabitants in the middle of the ocean. We kept repeating, "Turtle-shaped?" The Crown Prince answered, "Yes, turtle-shaped. Don't you know what a turtle is?" We shook our heads, oblivious of the knowledge. "Well, there are three members in the tortoise family," he began explaining. "There is a turtle. There is Tortoise, and there is Terrapins. All of which are reptiles. Do you guys know what a reptile is?" We nodded our heads.

"Good," he complimented. "So, Turtles live in the water and love swimming. Tortoises live on land and enjoy walking around slowly. Terrapins are like a mix of Turtles and Tortoises. They can live in both water and land but prefer the water most of the time. He explained the difference between the three members of the tortoise family. At that point, Alagba, the much-touted oldest and legendary tortoise who lived at the palace of the Soun of Ogbomoso, crossed my mind. Alagba died in October 2019. I thought of what would become his memory. He kindly addressed our concerns, but beyond the little animal kingdom, we were filled with admiration. Not for the knowledge he had but for his vision and determination to address the pressing challenges faced by individuals in need of organ transplants. Because he recognized the growing number of patients suffering from kidney failure and the immense impact it had on their lives, the king took proactive steps to establish the Saudi Center for Organ Transplantation. This groundbreaking initiative was designed to provide much-needed support and medical intervention to those on the organ transplant waiting list. The decision of King Salman and Crown Prince Mohammed bin Salman to personally register in the organ donor program resonated deeply with us. Their selflessness and compassion served as a powerful example for others to follow. By participating in the program, they not only highlighted the urgent need for organ donations but also emphasized the profound impact such donations could have on saving lives and providing hope to those in desperate circumstances. Their dedication and support for the Saudi Center for Organ Transplantation went beyond establishing the institution. They also actively engaged with the cause as they understood the critical importance of organ transplantation and the transformative effect it could have on individuals and their families. Their actions exemplified the values of empathy and care for their fellow citizens.

The unwavering commitment of King Salman and Crown Prince Mohammed bin Salman fostered a sense of unity and compassion within Saudi Arabia. Their endeavours created a culture where organ donation was recognised as a means of offering renewed chances at life and a lifeline of hope. Their visionary leadership ignited awareness and inspired others to consider organ donation as a selfless act with lasting impacts on the lives of those in need.

We informed people that the need for organs and tissue transplantation was becoming more urgent now that Coronavirus was ravaging the world and hospitals were being flooded with patients with multiple organ failure.

"We want you to be the face of our company?" one of the public relations managers of a well-known Nigerian pharmaceutical company told us as we reviewed a document we were given to read. The document said that we were being offered an endorsement worth a million dollars if we decided to become the face of their company and market their products by representing them at exhibitions. This was not the first or only company that contacted us.

Numerous companies approached us. Aanu was approached by an international company that manufactured hand-washing liquid. They wanted her to model in their company's public service advertisement, which would show people the importance of keeping complete hygiene in these troubled times. Aanu and I were bagging endorsements from all kinds of companies, but all the credit went to Ebun, who was resting in peace and marvelling at the chain reactions her selfless sacrifice initiated.

We became ambassadors of NGOs and went to rural and hard-to-reach areas in Nigeria to create awareness among people about the effects of Coronavirus and how to stop its spread. We were going on outreach programs every other day where we told Ebun's story and urged people to register themselves as organ donors.

"Wow, Ife, look!" Aanu exclaimed as our car sped past a huge billboard.

She pointed at the billboard; it had two big cutouts of Aanu and me with 'Ebun's vision' written in neon lights.

"This is all because of our sister," I told Aanu as I held her hand. "She is gone, but she is still making waves across the world."

We missed her dearly, and we were working tirelessly to make her vision a reality. Mum was equally proud of us as she heard people praising us for our philanthropic activities.

We both were generating huge sums of revenue in the form of endorsements by brands and pharmaceutical companies, donations, cheques as well as merchandise, all in the name of Ebun's vision. We managed to gather a large number of school supplies from a generous donor, who helped an NGO build a school in just a few weeks.

Aanu and I became messiahs of some sort to the general public. Everyone knew us. Wherever we went, people walked up to us, praised us, and asked for pictures and autographs. Ebun was smiling at us from heaven. Our dad smiled whenever he heard Ebun's name on the news or in the newspaper. Although his daughter was not in the world anymore, her name was everywhere.

Lisa and Ann helped to spread Ebun's vision, too. They would stream Ebun's old videos and ask for donations from viewers for 'Ebun's Vision,' which was an organisation in the making. Aanu and I were given a car gift from a wealthy anonymous philanthropist. The car came with a driver, so we could do charitable work without worrying about transport. Coronavirus was claiming lives, and Aanu and I were out saving as many as we could.

Never in our wildest imagination did we think that our lives would be thrust into the fast lane. However, when it happened, we did not flinch; rather, we took on the challenge without looking back. The public loved Aanu and me for filling the gap that our beloved sister had left.

In remembrance of Ebun, a statue was erected in front of the University

Teaching Hospital, Abuja. People left candles, posters, cards, and flowers in front of the statue and lit candles there every night.

People were coming together in the name of Ebun (Love). Everyone chanted, 'Ebun! Ebun!' whenever we arrived at an event. People would respond to our calls and come out to help with the charitable works we were doing in Lagos and adjoining areas. Lagos was severely hit by Coronavirus, and people were in extreme distress. With our efforts, we were able to establish a makeshift hospital in the poverty-stricken areas of Lagos, which was like an oasis.

There was a massive scarcity of oxygen cylinders as COVID-19 patients needed them the most. Meanwhile, people were getting infected at an alarming rate. In this dire situation, we collaborated with an industrial oxygen-making company, and as a result, we were able to provide free oxygen tanks to people who were in need.

Even though Aanu and I were just teenagers, we topped the list of people helping others out at this time. We had become A-list celebrities, and there was not a single person in Nigeria who did not know us or Ebun. We distributed the money we generated and invested some of it for social causes.

"We are doing all that we can. What else can we do to help people?" I asked Aanu when we returned home from another tiring day of distributing rations among needy people.

"Pray," Aanu said as she lay beside me for a good night's sleep. "We can pray that God sends a cure our way. A more practical approach will be saving more money so that when the time comes when we have a vaccine for this wretched disease, we can buy it. As we all know, countries are already eager to get their hands on the vaccine that is in the works. When the vaccine is produced, we should be ready to buy it and help people in Nigeria. That is what Ebun would have wanted."

CHAPTER 8 DISCUSSION QUESTIONS

1. How did the socio-economic repercussions of the COVID-19 crisis lead to increased criminal activity?

2. Discuss the implications of the almajiri system in light of the pandemic and its broader socio-cultural context.

3. What are the potential challenges of relying heavily on endorsements and donations during a crisis?

4. How did the socioeconomic repercussions of the COVID-19 crisis lead to increased criminal activities?

5. What was the Impact of King Salman and Crown Prince Mohammed bin Salman's Advocacy for Organ Donation in Saudi Arabia?

6. How did King Salman and Crown Prince Mohammed bin Salman's initiatives during the COVID-19 pandemic, particularly in relation to organ donation and transplantation, reflect their leadership and vision for the country's healthcare system?

CHAPTER 9

IFE

Our lives changed overnight. From school-going kids, we became A-list celebrities. We started earning money from endorsement deals and donations from philanthropists and organisations. Our parents told us that we were going to go places with the exposure we were getting but that we should never forget our roots and remain humble. Aanu and I loved and respected our mum very much. We promised her that no matter where we went, we were going to stay humble and not lose focus.

Our main focus was "Ebun's Vision" foundation, a non-governmental organisation in the making. We finally registered the name, but it lacked a physical campus. As donations and funds poured in, it was just a matter of weeks before we opened Ebun's Vision Foundation.

Coronavirus was getting contained slowly and gradually, first in developed countries and then in developing countries. China did not want to be left out, so they contacted us.

"Hi, am I talking to Mrs Olokun-Esin?" a woman asked over the phone.

"Yes, this is her. Who am I talking to?" she asked.

"My name is Chun," the woman introduced herself. "I am the Chief of Staff to the president of the People's Republic of China. We are so sorry to hear about your daughter's demise. She was our guest a few months back when the outbreak began. It was truly an honour to have her here, and sadly, she is not with us anymore. We have heard about the amazing work your daughters are doing. Mr President sends his regards. You have raised your kids right."

"I appreciate that. May I know the reason behind your call? I am sure you didn't call me just to condole with me."

"Certainly. I was asked to invite your daughters to China. The lockdown has been lifted, and the situation is under control now. The president would like to meet them along with some famous political and public figures of the country. We want Aanu and Ife to be our guests, and we want to give them a tour of Hong Kong, with your permission, of course," Chun told Mum.

"That is very generous of you. Tell the president that I appreciate his offer, and I will talk to my daughters and make a decision," Mum said.

Even though she knew that we would want to go and see the places our sister went before she died, she wanted to talk to her daughters first. She wanted us to decide for ourselves.

When she told us about it, we were pleasantly surprised, and she was happy when we asked for her permission to go to China. She was proud that we got a call from the president's office. According to her, that was an achievement in itself. She permitted us to go under the condition that we would stick together and take care of each other on our trip.

We agreed to the conditions and started preparing for the trip. We were happy; we had tears in our eyes. We felt we were making a pilgrimage to where our sister contracted a disease that led to her early death. When Ebun spoke about China, we remembered the sparkle in her eyes, and we wanted to relive it by visiting the places she was always talking about after she returned from China.

We packed our bags and gathered our documents. We were informed that a chartered plane that the Chinese government had provided would be taking us to China. Though Aanu and I were used to the royal treatment we got everywhere we went, this was by far our biggest royal treat.

When Aanu and I arrived in Beijing, we were received by officials from the president's office who gave us VIP treatment all the way to the hotel. We were given the Presidential Suite at the Aman Hotel and Resorts, which was one of the best in Beijing.

After months of working tirelessly, this was a much-needed break. We enjoyed a day at the spa and ate a lavish buffet. The next day, we visited all the sites that Ebun had told us about.

"Isn't this amazing?" Aanu asked me as she put her hand on my shoulder.

"It truly is. Ebun was right. Everyone should come here at least once in their lifetime to witness this wonder!" I cooed as we stood on the Great Wall of China and enjoyed the view. We had to climb what seemed like a million stairs to get to the Great Wall of China, which was not an easy feat. We also had to take a mountain cable car since the Great Wall of China was located on a mountain. Then, several additional stairs appeared. We were exhausted and drenched in sweat when, at last, we arrived atop the Great Wall of China. Despite our desire to rest and sit down, our eagerness prompted us to get up and start to walk.

After we were done sightseeing the Wall, we were taken to the 789 Art Zone, where we hung around for a while before we went to Tribe Solana and had food. We did everything that Ebun did in Beijing, including going to the Forbidden City. It was very emotional for us to see the places our beloved sister saw before passing away. It was as though we were retracing every inch of her golden steps. Knowing Ebun, we knew that she must have had so much fun when she came, and she missed us on that fateful trip. Now, it was our turn to miss her; we wished she was there with us.

Aanu and I were given a country-wide tour of China. We were taken care of like royalty and invited to Hong Kong. We were told that the Chinese government was throwing a ball in Ebun's honour and we were the chief guests.

We had been in meetings all day and were exhausted. As we were about to retire to our rooms, Aanu's phone rang. It was an unexpected call from an unknown Chinese number. Aanu hesitated for a moment before answering.

"Hello?" she said, her voice barely above a whisper.

"Hello, this is Ying Wei from the Chinese Government. I am calling to extend a formal invitation to you and Ife to attend a ball in honour of your deceased sister, Ebun," the voice at the other end of the line said.

Aanu was taken aback.

"We understand how difficult it must be for you and Ife to be away from home during this time, but we would be honoured if you could attend the ball in her memory," Ying continued.

We were touched by the gesture.

"Thank you. We will be honoured to attend," she said, tears welling up in her eyes.

We received gifts comprising dresses that we could wear to the ball. We were treated as celebrities. The ball was scheduled for the following day, and Aanu and I spent time preparing for the event. We arrived at the venue, a grand ballroom in one of the most prestigious hotels in Hong Kong. As we stepped out of the car, we were greeted by a group of Chinese officials who escorted us to our seats.

The ballroom was filled with people, all elegantly dressed in black and white. There was a sombre atmosphere but also a sense of reverence and respect. Aanu and I were seated at the head table, and a large portrait of Ebun hung behind us.

The crème-de-la-crème of China were in attendance. We met Zhao Wei there, a famous filmmaker, as well as Jack Ma and Jackie Chan, who did not need an introduction. Aanu and I were asked to come on stage and address the people who had come together to celebrate Ebun.

"Coronavirus changed the world as we know it," I addressed the eminent guests. "It made us realise that we all are a big family, and when it comes to it, we all must unite regardless of colour, cast or creed. China played an important role in curbing the spread of Coronavirus, and we would like to congratulate the Chinese people for persevering in these difficult times. We will rise above all the damage this vile virus has done. There is no hurdle we cannot overcome when we all work together. Xie Xie."

As I ended my speech, the crowd roared and applauded us while chanting, "Ebun! Ebun!" It was a moment that Aanu and I would never forget.

The health minister of China, who was present at the ball, came on stage after we ended our speech and announced that in honour of Ebun's work, the government of Nigeria would be one of the first

countries to receive the tester coronavirus vaccination. Aanu and I were excited to hear this news; we managed to get the most important inventory for Nigeria's healthcare system in advance and without spending a dime.

Throughout the evening, Aanu and I were moved by the speeches and tributes given in Ebun's honour. We listened intently as Chinese officials spoke of her kindness, generosity, and unwavering commitment to helping others.

As the evening drew to a close, Aanu and I were presented with a gift from the Chinese Government—a beautiful painting of Ebun captured at Disneyland. Tears streamed down our faces as we thanked the officials for their kindness and generosity.

We felt a deep sense of gratitude for the Chinese people and their willingness to honour our sister's memory. It was a moment we would never forget and one that strengthened our belief in the power of diplomacy and human kindness. As we met people and talked to them, we figured out that Ebun had become an international sensation. The ball featured various acrobatic acts and a musical concert that went on all night long. After the ball, we were both tired, so we decided to head back to our palatial residence.

During our time in China, we discovered that even Chinese companies wanted us to become their ambassadors. We figured that it was the best way for us to raise funds for "Ebun's Vision." So, after sightseeing and attending official dinners for a week, we began to attend meetings at different companies. Medical companies in China were pleading with us to be their brand ambassadors.

After many meetings and careful decision-making, Aanu and I bagged several deals, including one from Pfizer. Pfizer was in the first row of companies researching a cure for Coronavirus. After we became their ambassadors, they announced that a small percentage of the profit from their COVID-19 vaccine would go to our family to be used in fulfilment of Ebun's Vision.

"We did it, sis! We did it," I said excitedly as we lay in our bed, looking at the magnificent chandelier that hung over us.

"If it was not for Ebun, so many people would have been helpless. Our work does not stop here. We still have a long way to go for as long as misery thrives in our country. We will never rest," Aanu smiled as we closed our eyes only to wake up to take on another day.

CHAPTER 9 DISCUSSION QUESTIONS

1. How did the trip to China affect Aanu and Ife emotionally, especially considering it was a journey to the places their late sister, Ebun, had once visited? What were some of the emotions they experienced during the trip?

2. The chapter highlights the impact of diplomacy, personal connections, and kindness in their mission. How do you think these elements played a role in their mission with "Ebun's Vision" foundation and their work in general?

3. The chapter mentions the role of celebrities in raising funds and awareness for important causes. How do Aanu and Ife's experiences in China and their work as ambassadors for medical companies contribute to their philanthropic efforts?

4. Aanu and Ife talk about the importance of unity in the face of a global crisis, such as the COVID-19 pandemic. How can global cooperation and unity help in overcoming such challenges?

5. Reflect on how the chapter illustrates the enduring impact of Ebun's legacy on her family's mission. How does her memory continue to inspire and guide their actions and decisions?

CHAPTER 10

IFE

C hina was amazing in that it gave me insight into the life of the Chinese people. I thought of the cuisine, attractions, and history when we decided to travel to China. In addition to all of these factors, I found out that the Chinese people made China one of the most developed countries in the world. We were concerned that the culture gap would be too big for us. However, when we established friendships with some locals and our hosts, we got to know that the people of China are loving, disciplined, hardworking and efficient.

"Hey, Ife, I saw you crying earlier at the Art Zone. Is everything fine?" Fen asked. Fen was head of the delegation that was taking care of us in China. We were on our way to the venue of the Chinese Cultural Program for Children.

"Yea, yea, I am fine. It's all cool," I said, looking outside the window. I thought for a brief moment and turned to Fen.

"I was missing Ebun. I was looking at one of the sculptures that she loved when she was here, and it made me cry. I loved her so much. She was an amazing and kind soul. Not a day goes by when I do not miss her. We all are like that. In Nigeria, we value family a lot. We always stick together."

"I understand. I am sorry. I just wanted to know if everything is alright. I guessed that you must be missing her, and I thought to let you know that I can relate to what you are feeling," Fen said.

"And how is that, if I may ask?" I asked with genuine concern and care.

"I had a sister, and she was just 11 years old when she died. She fell prey to

Coronavirus two months ago," Fen said. "I miss her every day. When I

look at you two, I feel so much better. However, the thought of it makes me miss her more. Chinese people are very family-oriented, too, you see. We don't live together as a family because we are successful but because it is the preferred choice of all family members. In contrast to the more individualistic approach of the West, respect and close ties between parents and children are the norm in China."

"I didn't know that," I said in astonishment since I was unaware of his story. "In Nigeria, we also like to live in close-knit big families more than living individually and alone in Nigeria. I guess that's because we Nigerians are comfortable with each other."

The shared knowledge of loss between us and Fen lifted my mood somewhat and made me feel much better.

"Ah, so are we," Fen continued. "Chinese people are far more at ease in crowded spaces than other people, whether you blame it on the collectivist society or urbanisation. Foreigners frequently experience some form of claustrophobia in China, whether in a crowded metro, during a family reunion, or even when having random conversations at a table.

"At first, this may be unsettling. For instance, in the West, I would feel the need to apologise after running into someone in a crowd before moving on. In China, running into other individuals is so common that no one bothers to stop. This is hardly an act of rudeness. It's just a different set of manners that has been modified to reflect how the culture has evolved here."

"That is so cool. We have much more in common than our differences. You just shared a valuable piece of information with me. I will hold on to it. Xie Xie!" I said, smiling and shaking Fen's hand joyfully. Fen's smile showed his pearly whites, and he bowed in the traditional Chinese manner.

When we finally arrived at the venue of the Chinese Cultural Program for Children, I was excited and curious about what the day had in store for us. The place was adorned with vibrant decorations that showcased the richness of the Chinese culture.

As we mingled with other attendees, Aanu suddenly caught my attention. There in the crowd, she was engaged in an animated conversation with a teenager from Japan. The connection between them was undeniable; you could almost see sparks flying between both of them. From the way they exchanged smiles and shy glances, it was apparent that they both liked each other.

Intrigued, I watched as Aanu took the initiative to inquire about the girl's name.

"What's your name?" she asked with genuine interest. The Japanese girl replied, "I'm Yui Kuwabara."

Aanu was immediately curious about what Yui meant, to which she replied, "My name means excellence or superiority."

Aanu then complimented her, "What a lovely and meaningful name you have, Yui!"

Eager to share about herself as well, Aanu said, "My name is Aanu, which means Mercy."

But that wasn't all; she had a fascinating story to tell about her surname, Olokun-Esin. She explained its historical connection to a war general in the ancient Oyo Empire, ruled by Alaafins. She told Yui that her progenitor had the solemn duty to protect the empire, even at the cost of his life. When the emperor dies, whether by natural causes or otherwise, Olokun-Esin must follow him to the afterlife to demonstrate his loyalty and service. It meant that Olokun-Esin must commit suicide and be buried alongside the emperor.

Yui was taken aback by this ancient practice, and with concern in her eyes, she asked, "For real?"

Aanu solemnly confirmed, "Yes, that's how it was back then."

However, she quickly reassured Yui that times had changed and that the tradition was no longer in practice. The weight of that responsibility had been lifted, and future generations were free from such a burden. "It's truly a responsibility taken to the extreme," Yui remarked with a mix of shock and admiration. She couldn't fathom the sacrifice and dedication it demanded. Aanu nodded in agreement, acknowledging the heavy burden that her ancestors had shouldered. But at the same time, she was grateful that the practice had ended, which allowed her family and descendants to live without that haunting obligation.

As the day wore on, Aanu and Yui continued to bond and discover more about each other's cultures and backgrounds.

"The interesting history of your last name struck a chord," said Yui, her eyes shining with intrigue.

"Tell me, what chord?" Aanu demanded, her curiosity piqued by Yui's words.

Yui took a moment to collect her thoughts before sharing the powerful story of her family's past.

"Okay, this is a story from my family; my father was less than a year old when it all happened," she began. "It was February 3, 1975, when tragedy struck aboard a Japan Airlines Boeing 747 flying from

Anchorage, Alaska, to Copenhagen, Denmark. A total of 197 passengers fell ill after consuming a contaminated in-flight meal, resulting in the largest food poisoning incident on a commercial airliner to date. Among them, 144 people needed immediate hospitalisation."

Yui described how a United States Public Health Service investigation team diligently worked to find the source of the contamination.

"They conducted laboratory tests on stool and vomit samples from passengers and also on 33 samples of leftover ham omelettes," Yui explained. "The tests revealed the presence of staphylococcus aureus, and they also detected elevated concentrations of toxins in the ham, explaining the remarkably short incubation time."

The investigation focused on international in-flight catering facilities, specifically a subsidiary of Japan Airlines in Anchorage, where the meals had been prepared. Yiu's next words startled Aanu.

"They discovered that three cooks were responsible for preparing the contaminated meals, and one of them had infected lesions on his right hand. The lesions were infected with staphylococci, and tests showed that this cook was the source of the contamination.

"Incredibly, this suspect cook had prepared meals for three out of the four galleys on the aircraft," Yui continued. "He handled all 40

omelettes served in first class and 72 out of 108 for one of the main deck galleys. Furthermore, he prepared all 108 omelettes for another galley, totalling 220 meals."

Yui then revealed the tragic connection to her own family.

"My grandfather, Kenji Kuwabara, was the Vice President of international in-flight catering at the time," she said sombrely. "He was a 52-year-old man of great responsibility. When he learned that the incident was caused by one of his cooks, the weight of the tragedy was too much for him to bear. In the face of such a heavy burden, he made the heartbreaking decision to end his life."

Aanu listened intently, trying to quantify the immense honour and dedication her friend's grandfather had shown. She realised the profound impact that one's sense of responsibility could have on one's life and those around them.

"Wow, your grandfather must have been a man of true honour," Aanu said, deeply impressed by the sacrifices he had made.

"Yes, he was," Yui replied, her voice filled with pride and sadness. "His story reminds me of the importance of responsibility and safety in the food industry and the devastating consequences that can arise from neglecting such matters." As they sat together, Yui and Aanu shared a moment of mutual respect for their family histories and the lessons they had learned.

Through their stories, they discovered the strength and resilience that ran deep in their bloodlines, connecting them in a profound and meaningful way. The Chinese Cultural Program had not only brought them together to appreciate each other's cultures but had also forged a bond rooted in shared experiences and understanding.

As the Chinese Cultural Program came to a close, there was a touching tribute video dedicated to our beloved sister, Ebun. It showcased her selfless act of donating her organs, which had a profound impact not only locally but internationally as well. Ebun's last wish sparked a social movement, inspiring countless individuals around the world to consider organ donation as a way to save lives and leave a lasting legacy of kindness and compassion.

The video captured the essence of Ebun's vibrant personality, her passion for life, and her unwavering commitment to making a positive difference. It was a bittersweet moment as we celebrated her life and the remarkable impact she had on so many people.

After the emotional tribute, we returned to the mansion we were lodged in for the duration of our stay. The mansion was a grand and elegant structure, reflecting the cultural richness of the city we were visiting. It provided a comfortable and inviting space for us to rest and reflect on the incredible experiences we shared during the program.

As we settled into our rooms, we reminisced about the meaningful connections we made with people from different cultures and backgrounds. The memories of the Chinese Cultural Program will forever hold a special place in our hearts, not only because of the cultural exchange and educational experiences but also because of the tribute to our dear sister, Ebun.

In the days that followed, we continued to engage in activities and discussions that fostered stronger bonds. The mansion became a place of laughter, learning, and heartfelt conversations that deepened our understanding and appreciation of one another.

As we prepared to depart, we knew that the impact of this journey would stay with us forever. The international social movement ignited by Ebun's last wish would continue to grow and touch countless lives, reminding us of the power of kindness and the importance of leaving a positive mark on the world.

With grateful hearts and cherished memories, we bid farewell to the mansion and the city that had become our temporary home. As Aanu and I got ready for our flight home after two weeks of exploring China and bagging endorsement deals, we received the news that all of the surgeries that were made possible due to the donation of Ebun's organs had been completed successfully. All the recipients sent their regards and love to Ebun and her family.

As people in different countries thanked Ebun for her bravery and generosity through social media, the media started interviewing the recipients. Afterward, they shared their stories with the public. Some asked them about their experience and what they thought about Ebun, while others interviewed their families to ask how grateful they were for Ebun's sacrifice.

Aanu and I were being interviewed before and after we became celebrities. News channels were running video packages on Ebun and her life on different channels and streaming platforms. There was even a Netflix documentary on Ebun in the works.

As the news spread like wildfire, donations started pouring in from all over the world. Officials of the Saudi Government urged their people to donate to this great cause, and so did everyone who received Ebun's donation.

The main goal of this foundation was to provide and receive donations and grants for organ transplants in fulfilment of Ebun's dying wish. At first, the foundation was a general hospital and an office for charitable works, but soon, construction started for a 1,000-bedroom organ and tissue transplant centre. It was named "The Ebun Centre," and it was built in Abuja, Nigeria.

Aanu and I started a campaign through Ebun's foundation. The campaign's main goal was to get both the government and the people involved in the issue of organ transplantation so that the government could give genuine people relief. In return, the government earned the public's trust. Aanu and I invited Mr President to the opening ceremony of "The Ebun Centre."

The government approved and appreciated our initiative and promised to help The Ebun Centre with anything we required. The President of Nigeria attended the opening ceremony as promised while holding the article that inspired Ebun. Mr President encouraged children to read, be curious, and ask difficult questions. In his address, he told the people that if a small child like Ebun could make such a huge difference, millions of Nigerians would bring amazing change if they worked together selflessly.

Soon after construction, The Ebun Centre was up and running. It provided free organ transplants to all Nigerians, irrespective of their financial status and or where they came from. Aanu and I managed the facility with passion and dedication. Our main motivator was our love for Ebun and her dream. Over time, The Ebun Centre evolved into a 3,000-bed hospital that adhered strictly to international health standards.

It had been only a few months, and The Ebun Centre had evolved into something bigger than anyone originally imagined. It did not only specialise in transplant surgeries. Soon, the need arose for expansion, and we started building a separate hospital for cancer and terminally ill patients, too.

Since we needed qualified Nigerian medical staff, we persuaded all Nigerian medical workers who had left for better opportunities abroad to return. We offered them better salaries than the ones they received in their respective overseas countries. Within a month after our call for help, a large number of doctors and medical personnel returned to work at The Ebun Centre.

The Ebun Centre was not only taking care of people's health for free, but it was also creating jobs for unemployed people. The Ebun Centre soon became an inspiration for the Nigerian Government. In recognition of

Ebun's vision, as promised, the government took radical steps by allocating 15% of the budget to healthcare.

Ebun had done it! She had become immortalised. She had made a difference and cemented her place as a legend and a public figure in the medical world, like Florence Nightingale and Marie Curie. And that was how Ebun Olokun-Esin became the pride of Nigeria.

CHAPTER 10 DISCUSSION QUESTIONS

1. How did the international social movement inspired by Ebun's organ donation impact people around the world, and what kind of response did it receive?

2. Describe the development and purpose of the "The Ebun Centre" in Abuja, Nigeria. How did it contribute to organ transplantation and healthcare in the country?

3. How did Aanu and Ife manage The Ebun Centre, and what motivated their dedication to this facility?

4. What were the long-term effects of Ebun's vision and the foundation's work on healthcare and employment in Nigeria?

5. How did the Nigerian government respond to the initiative of Aanu and Ife, and what steps did they take to support healthcare in the country?

6. In what ways did Ebun become immortalised and recognised as a legend and public figure in the medical world, and why is her legacy compared to figures like Florence Nightingale and Marie Curie?

7. How would you describe the overall impact of Ebun Olokun-Esin's story and the narrative's message or themes?

www.ingramcontent.com/pod-product-compliance
Lightning Source LLC
Chambersburg PA
CBHW051532120626
46551CB00012B/1186